FlashKids SUMMER

3rd Grade

Jumpstart third grade with fun skill-building activities!

FlashKids
New York

New York

An Imprint of Sterling Publishing Co., Inc.

ISBN 978-1-4114-8066-7

Distributed in Canada by Sterling Publishing Co., Inc.
c/o Canadian Manda Group, 664 Annette Street
Toronto, Ontario, M6S 2C8, Canada
Distributed in the United Kingdom by GMC Distribution Services
Castle Place, 166 High Street, Lewes, East Sussex, BN7 1XU, England
Distributed in Australia by NewSouth Books
University of New South Wales, Sydney, NSW 2052, Australia

For information about custom editions, special sales, and premium
and corporate purchases, please contact Sterling Special Sales
at specialsales@sterlingpublishing.com.

Manufactured in Malaysia
Lot #:
2 4 6 8 10 9 7 5 3 1
11/21

sterlingpublishing.com

Cover illustration: Justin Poulter

Front cover image: monkeybusinessimages/iStock/Getty Images Plus
Back cover image: leolintang/iStock Getty Images Plus
All interior images by Depositphotos, iStockphoto, Shutterstock, Thinkstock,
and Wikimedia Foundation with the following exception: © Dorling Kindersley/
Getty Images (map); Science Source: ©Millard H. Sharp (whooping crane),
©Helen Williams (white winged duck).

Dear Caregiver,

As a caregiver, you want your child to have time to relax and have fun during the summer, but you don't want your child's math and reading skills to get rusty. How do you make time for summer fun while ensuring that your child will be ready for the next school year?

The *Flash Kids Summer* workbook provides short, fun activities to help children keep their skills fresh all summer long. This book not only reviews what students learned during second grade, it also introduces what they'll be learning in third grade. Best of all, the games, puzzles, and stories help students retain their knowledge as well as build new skills. By the time your child finishes the book, they will be ready for a smooth transition into the next school year.

As your child completes the activities in this book, shower them with encouragement and praise. You can feel good knowing that you are taking an active and important role in your child's education. Helping your child complete the activities in this book is providing an excellent example—that you value learning every day! Have a wonderful summer, and most of all have fun learning together!

Wonderful Watermelons

Add the numbers on the slices of watermelon. The first one is done for you.

1.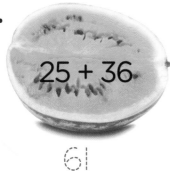
25 + 36

_61_

2.
21 + 33

_____

3.
56 + 87

_____

4.
41 + 59

_____

5.
73 + 44

_____

6.
82 + 83

_____

7.
121 + 232

_____

8.
345 + 459

_____

9.
654 + 127

_____

10.
555 + 350

_____

11.
732 + 246

_____

12.
403 + 197

_____

Picture Day

A **noun** names a person, place, or thing. Read the story. On each line, write a noun to name the picture. Use the words in the box to help you.

hunter	bird	tree	woods	ant
heart	foot	leaf	stream	stick

One day, a little _____ went for a drink. As he was

drinking, he fell into the _____ ! He held onto a

_____ but he fell back into the water. In a _____

above, a _____ saw the little ant drowning! She flew down

with a _____ and pulled Ant to shore. Ant was very thankful!

Later that day, a _____ saw Bird in the tree. He set a

trap to catch her. Ant saw what the hunter planned to do.

As the hunter came close, Ant bit him on the _____ .

The hunter ran away into the _____ . Bird thanked Ant

for his big _____ ."One good deed deserves another," Ant said.

School Is Out!

Look at the numbers on each bus. Use the numbers to write four math facts below each bus.

6, 9, 15

6 + 9 = 15
9 + 6 = 15
15 - 6 = 9
15 - 9 = 6

4, 7, 11

_____
_____
_____
_____

6, 7, 13

_____
_____
_____
_____

5, 4, 9

_____
_____
_____
_____

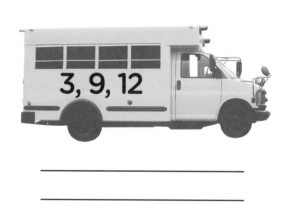

3, 9, 12

_____
_____
_____
_____

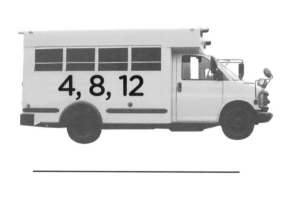

4, 8, 12

_____
_____
_____
_____

Bubble-Blowing Contest!

Subtract the numbers on the bubbles. Circle the bubble with the greatest difference in each row.

17 – 9
8
____

36 – 27
9
____

53 – 49
4
____

86 – 42
____

73 – 51
____

69 – 33
____

101 – 43
____

135 – 102
____

247 – 168
____

930 – 642
____

875 – 250
____

444 – 309
____

Number Hunt

Count by twos, starting with **2**. Circle each number. Count by fives, starting with **5**. Cross out each number. Some numbers will be circled <u>and</u> crossed out.

1	(2)	3	4	5̶	6	7	8	9	10
11	12	13	14	15	16	17	18	19	20
21	22	23	24	25	26	27	28	29	30
31	32	33	34	35	36	37	38	39	40
41	42	43	44	45	46	47	48	49	50
51	52	53	54	55	56	57	58	59	60
61	62	63	64	65	66	67	68	69	70
71	72	73	74	75	76	77	78	79	80
81	82	83	84	85	86	87	88	89	90
91	92	93	94	95	96	97	98	99	100

Write ten numbers you name when counting by both twos and fives.

10 ____ ____ ____ ____

____ ____ ____ ____ ____

Summer Sentences

Answer the questions below.

A sentence is a group of words that tells a complete idea.
For example, this is a sentence:

The sun is shining.

A group of words that does not tell a complete idea is **not** a
sentence. For example, this is not a sentence:

The sun.

Read each group of words. Circle the sentences.

1. (We're having a party.)
2. Swimming in the pool.
3. Lots of music.
4. Everyone will dance.
5. Swimming races and diving contests.
6. We will serve burgers and chips.
7. We hope you can come.
8. Stamps for the invitations.

Read the groups of words below. Add words to make your own sentences.

9. the bright sun

_____

_____

10. on a hot day

_____

_____

Counting Adjectives

Adjectives are describing words. Find and circle the adjectives in each sentence. Write the number of adjectives you circled on the line.

1. Jun found (six)(pink) shells in the (hot) sand. _3_

2. Ten students painted a huge colorful mural on the wall. ___

3. I gave one striped kitten to my teacher. ___

4. Manuel is tall with brown hair and green eyes. ___

5. Dad built a yellow playhouse in the backyard. ___

6. Small furry bunnies hopped across the park. ___

7. The sour milk left a bad taste in my mouth. ___

8. My sweet little sister made Mom a funny card. ___

9. This is the best cake I've ever tasted! ___

10. Red and yellow leaves covered the ground. ___

Magnet Mania

Magnets push and pull on certain objects.
They can also push and pull other magnets.

Find out what kinds of objects are attracted to magnets.
Find a magnet and collect the items in the list below.

crayon   metal paper clip

plastic straw   belt buckle

scissors   paper cup

metal measuring spoon

Hold the magnet next to each item. Write the names of the items
that stick to the magnet on the lines below.

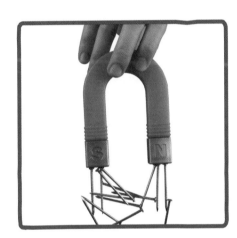

1. _____

2. _____

3. _____

4. _____

Lots of people use magnets to stick papers and notes on their refrigerators.
Design a magnet for your refrigerator. Draw a picture of your
magnet on the refrigerator below.

Tricky Time

Look at the time on each clock to the left.
Draw a line to the matching time phrase on the right.

twelve o'clock

quarter past ten

eleven twenty

half past seven

ten to nine

six forty

three forty-five

ten after five

Story Order

Write numbers **1** to **5** to put the events of each story in correct order.

1. ____ He broke his leash and chased the cat.

   ____ Oh no, Kip saw a cat!

   ____ First, we put him on his leash.

   ____ It was time to take Kip to the park.

   ____ Then we started walking to the park.

2. ____ Mia wanted something to eat.

   ____ Then she opened the jam jar.

   ____ Yum! Mia's muffin was good!

   ____ She spread jam on the muffin.

   ____ First, she took out a muffin and jam.

3. ____ Jack jumped onto the bus.

   ____ Jack got up late.

   ____ Then he put on his coat and backpack.

   ____ He ran to the bus.

   ____ First, he rushed to eat and get dressed.

A Shirt for Dad

It's Father's Day! Number the sentences in order from **1** to **6** to show the steps involved in getting Dad a shirt for his special day.

_____ The fabric is sent to a factory.

_____ The customer wraps the shirt and gives it to Dad on Father's Day.

_____ The shirt is sold to a store.

_____ Workers at the factory cut and sew the fabric to make the shirt.

_____ Cotton is grown, harvested, and turned into fabric.

_____ The store sells the shirt to a customer.

Color the shirt below to make a design that you like.

Take Off

Look at the chart to see what time the planes leave the airport.

FLIGHT GOING TO	LEAVES AT
Denver	6:15 AM
New York	7:15 AM
Seattle	10:45 AM
Chicago	12:30 PM
New Orleans	1:30 PM
Los Angeles	2:45 PM

Draw hands on the clocks to show the times the flights leave.
The first one is done for you.

1.

Denver

2.
New York

3.
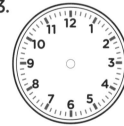
Seattle

4.

Chicago

5.

New Orleans

6.

Los Angeles

Guess the Coins

Write the value of each coin to solve the problems.

 = 1¢   = 5¢   = 10¢    = 25¢

1. Kara found four coins under the bed.
They are worth 50¢.
What coins did she find?

25¢ 10¢ 10¢ 5¢

2. Danny has five coins in his bank.
He has 95¢.
What coins are in his bank?

___ ___ ___ ___ ___

3. Bianca has five coins in her pack.
She has 26¢.
What coins are in her pack?

___ ___ ___ ___ ___

4. Tim has four coins in his hand.
They are worth 80¢.
What coins does he have?

___ ___ ___ ___

Rhyme Time

Read the first word in each row. Then circle the word that rhymes with it.

1. true	trip	(blew)	spell	door
2. white	stall	when	fly	bite
3. back	track	bake	king	break
4. dust	drink	rust	like	trunk
5. swing	store	quit	swap	thing
6. feet	seal	street	frog	sing
7. stop	stick	sink	drop	coat
8. lake	look	hand	brake	black

Now help Misty find her mouse. Draw lines between the circled words.

Island Shopper

Marcy is going to Hawaii with her family. She wants to buy some souvenirs.
Circle the bills and coins she needs for each gift.

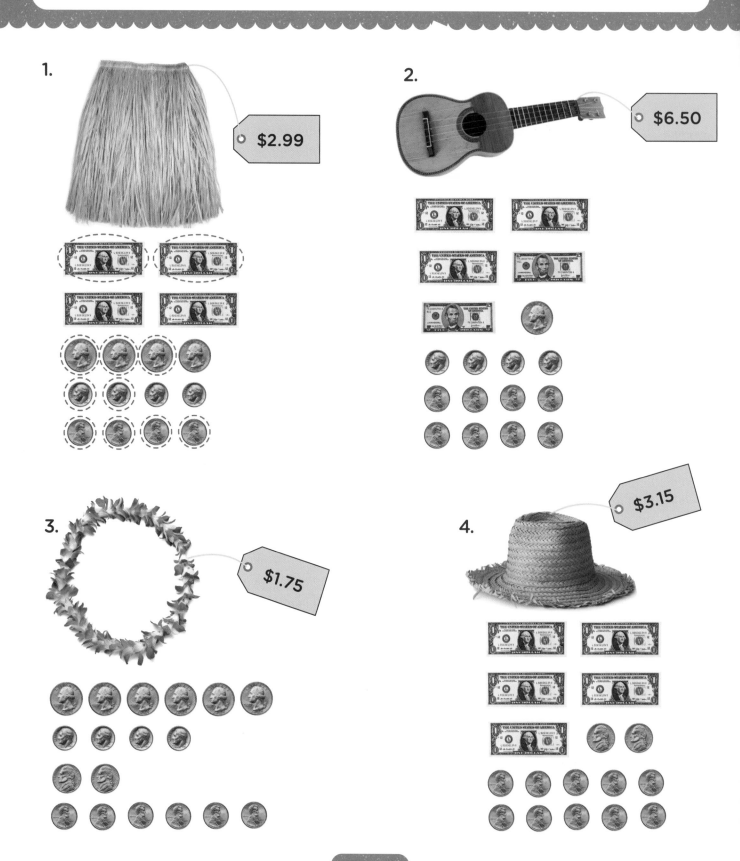

1. $2.99

2. $6.50

3. $1.75

4. $3.15

Sailing with Synonyms

Synonyms are words that mean the same thing.
Read the words on the sails. Write a synonym for each word.

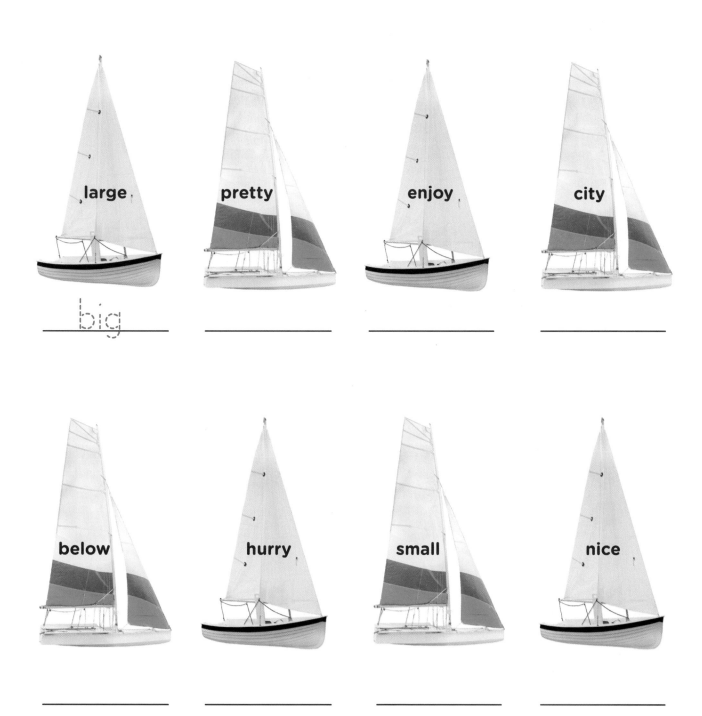

large

big
_____

pretty
_____

enjoy
_____

city
_____

below
_____

hurry
_____

small
_____

nice
_____

Busy Bugs

Circle the bugs to show each fraction.

Example:

The circled bugs represent $\dfrac{1}{4}$ of the total.

1.

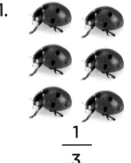

$\dfrac{1}{3}$

2.

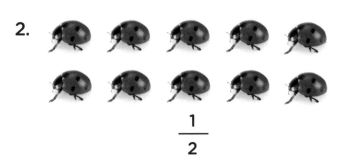

$\dfrac{1}{2}$

3.

$\dfrac{3}{4}$

4.

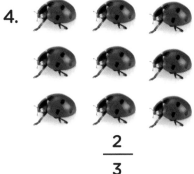

$\dfrac{2}{3}$

5.

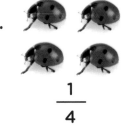

$\dfrac{1}{4}$

6.

$\dfrac{1}{2}$

Mix and Match

Draw a line matching each word to its abbreviation.

Jan.	Doctor	Sr.	Thursday
Sun.	Friday	Apr.	Missus
Nov.	Sunday	Aug.	April
Tues.	Mister	Mon.	Monday
Dr.	Junior	Mrs.	Saturday
Feb.	January	Oct.	August
Mr.	November	Thurs.	Wednesday
Sept.	February	Sat.	October
Jr.	Tuesday	Dec.	Senior
Fri.	September	Wed.	December

Which Way?

A **prefix** is a small group of letters added to the beginning of a word.
A prefix changes the meaning of the word.

Prefix	Meaning	Example
pre-	before	pre + pay = prepay
un-	not, the opposite	un + pack = unpack
re-	again, back	re + play = replay

Rewrite each sentence. Change the underlined word or words that
have the prefixes of **pre-**, **un-**, or **re-**.

1. Mom <u>traced</u> our route on the map again.

   Mom retraced our route on the map.

2. The directions to the lack were <u>not clear</u>.

   _____

3. Then Dad <u>placed</u> the map <u>back</u> into his backpack.

   _____

4. Mom and Dad were <u>not happy</u> about being lost on the trail.

   _____

5. "We should have <u>viewed</u> our route <u>before</u>," said Mom.

   _____

6. "You're right," said Dad. "We are <u>not prepared</u> for this."

   _____

Sunny San Diego

Books have many parts. The **table of contents** is near the beginning of a book.
It tells you the name and page number for each chapter in the book.
A table of contents can help you find information in a book quickly.

This is a table of contents from a book about San Diego, California.
Read the table. Then answer the questions.

1. What chapter tells about hotels?
   Chapter 2

2. What chapter would you read if you wanted to learn what San Diego was like long ago?

3. On what page does Chapter 5 begin?

4. What kind of information would you find in Chapter 3?

5. What information begins on page 51?

6. What is the name of the chapter that tells about baseball games?

7. On what page does the index begin?

8. The San Diego Zoo is located in Balboa Park. Which chapter would you read to find out about the zoo?

How Many Acorns?

The squirrel has fifteen acorns. In each problem it eats a different number of acorns. Tell how many acorns are left. Write the subtraction problem on the line.

1.

$$\underline{15} - \underline{4} = \underline{11}$$

2.

$$\underline{} - \underline{} = \underline{}$$

3.

$$\underline{} - \underline{} = \underline{}$$

4.

$$\underline{} - \underline{} = \underline{}$$

5.

$$\underline{} - \underline{} = \underline{}$$

6.

$$\underline{} - \underline{} = \underline{}$$

7.

$$\underline{} - \underline{} = \underline{}$$

8.

$$\underline{} - \underline{} = \underline{}$$

Crazy Caves

Rocks are formed from materials called minerals. Limestone is a type of rock that is made from a mineral. Many caves are made from limestone. Read the journal entry about a trip to the Carlsbad Caverns. Then answer the questions.

June 28

Today we went to the Carlsbad Caverns. This is a whole chain of underground caves. The park ranger told us that the caves started forming millions of years ago. Rain water and minerals mixed and seeped through cracks in the ground to carve caves out of the limestone. Rocks called stalactites hang down from the roof of the caves. They look like giant icicles. Other rocks, the stalagmites, stick up out of the ground. Tomorrow, we're going to the deepest part of the caverns on the King's Palace tour.

1. What is the name of the caves that the author visited?

   The Carlsbad Caverns

2. How long ago did the caves begin to form?

   _____

3. What kind of rock are the caves made of?

   _____

4. What is the name of a rock formation that hangs down from the roof of a cave?

   _____

5. How do you think the author feels visiting the Carlsbad Caverns?

   _____

Dig the Dinos

Dinosaurs lived long ago. Match the picture of the dinosaur to its description.

Apatosaurus

This is a plant-eating dinosaur. It has a very long neck and a tail that can be used like a whip.

Stegosaurus

This is a plant-eating dinosaur. It has spikes on its tail to use as a weapon. It has plates on its back for protection.

Tyrannosaurus rex

This is a meat-eating dinosaur. It is very large, but it has small arms.

Triceratops

This is a plant-eating dinosaur. It has three horns on its head.

Compsognathus

This is a meat-eating dinosaur. It is about the size of a chicken.

Spelling with A

Circle the correct spelling of each word. Then find and circle the words in the word search. Words can go up, down, or diagonally.

1. whale	whalle	6. waist	wast
2. stain	stane	7. chane	chain
3. playd	played	8. snak	snake
4. awey	away	9. train	trane
5. today	tooday	10. brayn	brain

```
E  S  R  U  L  E  S  B  I  P
R  P  L  A  Y  E  D  R  T  L
T  R  C  W  H  E  A  A  L  S
H  A  A  H  A  U  Y  I  O  N
B  Y  T  R  A  I  N  N  S  A
O  I  H  O  Y  I  E  V  T  K
Y  N  E  A  D  H  N  S  A  E
H  E  W  U  D  A  I  I  I  E
N  A  G  O  I  A  Y  A  N  Q
A  E  G  Y  W  H  A  L  E  C
```

In the Air with Amelia

Read the story. Then answer the questions.

Amelia Earhart was born on July 24, 1897. She was different from other girls her age. She enjoyed climbing trees and playing baseball. She rode horses, went fishing, and caught frogs and toads. She even helped build a roller coaster in her grandparents' yard. Amelia was smart and brave. When she grew up, she became one of the first female pilots. She was the first woman to ever fly alone across the Atlantic Ocean, but she had an even bigger dream. Amelia wanted to fly all the way around the world along the equator. No one—man or woman—had ever done that before. Amelia set out to follow her dream. Sadly though, her plane was lost near the end of her journey. No one knows for sure what happened to Amelia, but most people think that her plane crashed into the ocean. Amelia Earhart's bravery still inspires people today.

Circle the sentences below that are **true**.
Cross out the sentences that are **false**.

1. Amelia helped build a roller coaster.

2. Amelia liked to sit quietly.

3. Amelia flew airplanes.

4. Amelia drove a car across the Atlantic Ocean.

5. Amelia wanted to fly around the globe.

6. People think that Amelia's plane crashed.

Camp Summerland

Welcome to Camp Summerland! Compare the numbers in each canoe.
Write **<**, **>**, or **=** between the numbers.

1. 34 < 43

2. 13 ◯ 31

3. 16 ◯ 27

4. 25 ◯ 35

5. 451 ◯ 154

6. 1,000 ◯ 999

7. 333 ◯ 343

8. 987 ◯ 789

9. 24 ◯ 11 + 13

10. 300 ◯ 200 + 200

11. 53 ◯ 5 + 30

12. 500 ◯ 250 + 25

Comparing Numbers

Which is more? Which is less? Finish each sentence
by writing **more** or **less** on the line.

1. 15 – 5 is __less__ than 2 + 9.

2. 10 + 9 is _____ than 29 – 12.

3. 22 – 10 is _____ than 9 + 6.

4. 25 + 6 is _____ than 13 + 19.

5. 33 – 8 is _____ than 45 – 22.

6. 20 + 20 is _____ than 15 + 21.

7. 50 – 27 is _____ than 30 + 11.

8. 62 + 27 is _____ than 55 + 38.

9. 46 + 17 is _____ than 28 + 32.

10. 77 – 41 is _____ than 18 + 27.

11. 86 – 43 is _____ than 90 – 45.

12. 39 – 16 is _____ than 23 + 31.

13. 98 – 66 is _____ than 58 – 28.

14. 39 + 33 is _____ than 26 + 50.

15. 44 + 19 is _____ than 31 + 37.

16. 55 – 12 is _____ than 68 – 27.

Pizza Party

It's Pizza Night at Camp Summerland. If all the campers living in one cabin will get the same amount of pizza, how many pieces of pizza does each camper get?

1. The Antelope Cabin has 6 campers.
Each camper will get __2__ pieces of pizza.

2. The Bobcat Cabin has 8 campers.
Each camper will get _____ pieces of pizza.

3. The Cheetah Cabin has 5 campers.
Each camper will get _____ pieces of pizza.

4. The Donkey Cabin has 4 campers.
Each camper will get _____ pieces of pizza.

5. In which cabin do the campers get the fewest slices of pizza?

_____

6. In which two cabins do the campers get the same number of slices of pizza?

_____

Playful Patterns

The Summerland Campers are stringing beads to make necklaces.
Help them finish the necklaces. Fill in the missing numbers.

1. — 5 – 7 – 9 – 11 – 13 – 15 – 17 – 19 —

2. — 2 – 4 – 8 – ___ – ___ – 64 – ___ – ___ —

3. — 4 – 8 – ___ – ___ – 20 – 24 – ___ – ___ —

4. — 35 – ___ – 45 – 50 – ___ – 60 – 65 – 70 —

5. — 150 – 200 – ___ – 300 – 350 – ___ – ___ – 500 —

6. — 90 – ___ – 70 – ___ – 50 – ___ – 30 – 20 —

7. — ___ – 21 – 18 – ___ – 12 – 9 – ___ – 3 —

8. — 410 – 400 – ___ – 380 – ___ – 360 – ___ – 340 —

Ounces or Pounds?

We use **ounces** to measure the weight of light objects. We use **pounds** to measure the weight of heavy objects. Look at each object. Would you use ounces or pounds to weigh it? Circle your answer.

1.

ounces   (pounds)

2.

ounces   pounds

3.

ounces   pounds

4.

ounces   pounds

5.

ounces   pounds

6.

ounces   pounds

7.

ounces   pounds

8.

ounces   pounds

9.

ounces   pounds

Creepy Crawly Spiders

Read the story. Then answer the questions below.

Are you scared of spiders? Some people say they are. But most spiders do not bite or harm people. They are very helpful animals. Here are some fun facts about spiders.

- **Spiders are not insects. They are arachnids.**
- **Spiders have eight legs and eight eyes.**
- **Spiders use their sticky webs to catch food. Most spiders eat insects.**
- **Spiders wrap their eggs in silk sacs.**
- **Baby spiders are called spiderlings.**
- **Tarantulas are the biggest spiders. They can grow up to 10 inches long!**
- **Tarantulas can eat beetles, frogs, and even birds!**
- **Spiders help people by eating harmful insects.**

1. What are spiders?

_____

2. What do most spiders eat?

_____

3. What are baby spiders called?

_____

4. How do spiders help people?

_____

Splish, Splash!

Antonyms are words that have opposite meanings.

Circle the antonym for the underlined word in each sentence.

1. It was a <u>warm</u> day at Camp Summerland.   cool   clear

2. The children <u>ran</u> to the pool.   skated   walked

3. Justin climbed the ladder for the <u>high</u> dive.   sky   low

4. When he jumped into the water, he made a <u>loud</u> splash.   quiet   wide

5. Soon, there were <u>many</u> children swimming in the pool.   few   several

Read the words below. Write an antonym for each one.

6. soft _____   7. first _____

8. wide _____   9. left _____

10. different _____   11. happy _____

Dear Friend

Write a letter to a friend telling him or her all about your summer.

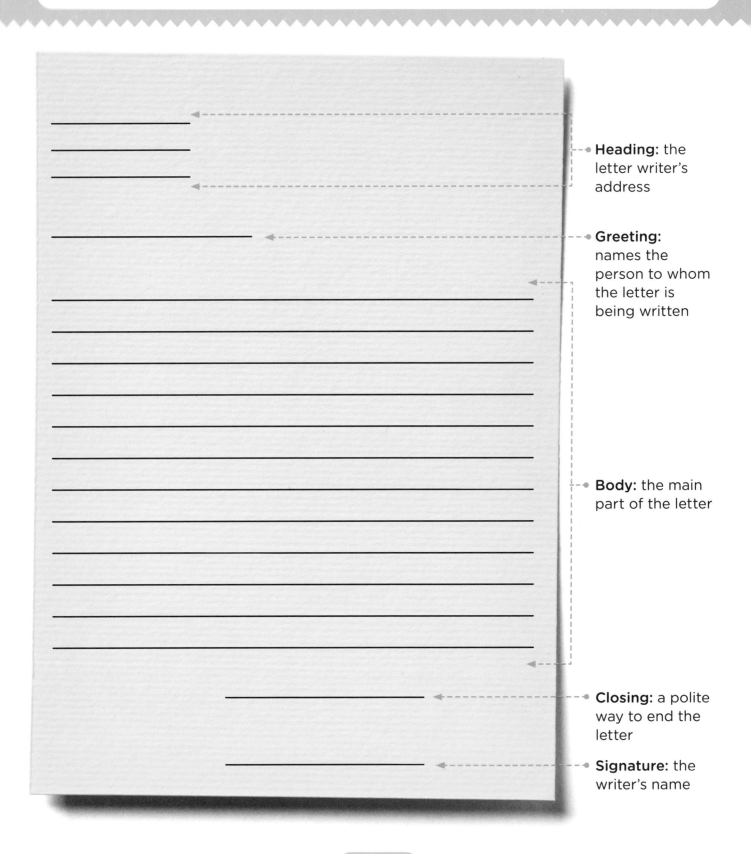

Heading: the letter writer's address

Greeting: names the person to whom the letter is being written

Body: the main part of the letter

Closing: a polite way to end the letter

Signature: the writer's name

Target Practice

Circle the two numbers in each target that add up to the target number.

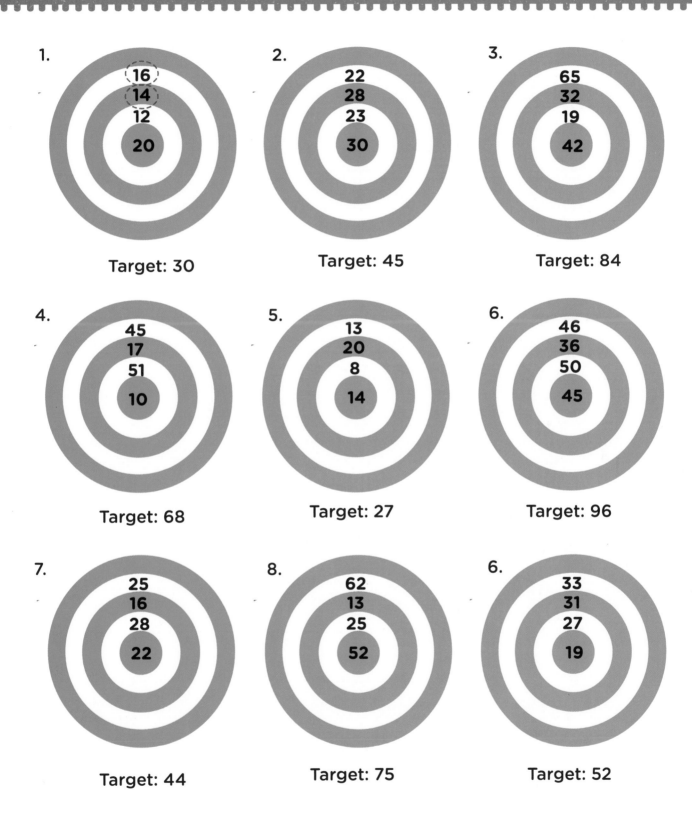

1.
16
14
12
20

Target: 30

2.
22
28
23
30

Target: 45

3.
65
32
19
42

Target: 84

4.
45
17
51
10

Target: 68

5.
13
20
8
14

Target: 27

6.
46
36
50
45

Target: 96

7.
25
16
28
22

Target: 44

8.
62
13
25
52

Target: 75

6.
33
31
27
19

Target: 52

Pen Pal

Follow the directions below.

This letter has a lot of mistakes! Fix the letter by:
- adding capital letters
- adding commas (,)
- adding ending punctuation (. ? !)

Hint: you should find 22 mistakes.

Example: ꭓ̶Hanna saw pink, white, and silver shells⊙

July 10, 2006

Dear kim

I am having a great time at the beach My dogs rex and Lad came too I saw starfish crabs, and fish in the tide pools. Did you know that a starfish can grow a whole new leg

The water here is warm and blue. dad says he will teach me to surf. Isn't that great i can't wait

My sisters Lisa and ana saw a whale today I wish I had seen it too they said the tail was as big as our car. Wow

I hope you are having a great summer i'll see you soon.

your friend
manuel

The Circle of Life

Number the sentences from **1** to **5** to show the
life cycle of a butterfly and a frog.

_____ Inside the chrysalis, the caterpillar's body begins to change.

_____ When the chrysalis opens up, a butterfly comes out.

_____ The caterpillar hangs itself from a twig and forms a chrysalis.

_____ A caterpillar hatches from an egg.

_____ As the caterpillar eats and grows, it sheds its skin.

_____ A frog egg is laid in water.

_____ When the tail is completely gone, it has turned into a frog.

_____ A tadpole begins to form inside the egg.

_____ The tail starts to shrink and legs begin to grow.

_____ The tadpole hatches from the egg with a tail and no legs.

Solve It!

Solve each problem. Write your answer on the line.

1.

Min saw 18 butterflies. Nine had purple wings. How many did not have purple wings? _____

2.

Ben's quilt has 12 squares. He has one more quilt just like it. How many squares are on both quilts? _____

3.

Jamie has 3 toy cars. Each car has 4 wheels. How many wheels are on all 3 cars? _____

4.

Emma has 20 goldfish. She put 12 in a pond. How many fish are left in the bowl? _____

5.

Josh has a bag of 35 candies. He gave away 15 pieces. How many pieces are left? _____

6.

Mina played with 10 kittens. Half of the kittens were striped. How many kittens were not striped? _____

Making Words

A **compound word** is a word made up of two other words. Draw a line from words on the left to words on the right to make compound words. Then write each new word on the line.

★ + 🐟 = ⭐
star + fish = starfish

1. snow — card   (S) n o w f l a k e

2. door — shell   _ _ _ _ _ (_) _ _ _

3. sea — cake   _ _ (_) _ _ _ _

4. key — knob   (_) _ _ _ _ _ _ _

5. bare — lace   _ _ _ (_) _ _ _ _

6. post — flake   _ _ (_) _ _ _ _

7. shoe — shine   _ (_) _ _ _ _ _

8. pea — foot   _ _ (_) _ _ _

9. pan — nut   _ _ _ _ _ (_) _

10. sun — board   _ _ _ _ _ _ _ (_)

Write the circled letters in order to solve the riddle:

What do you call a reptile dessert?

__ __ __ __ __   __ __ __ __ __

Hello, Daddy-O!

At Camp Summerland, grandparents are invited to visit for a day. The campers decorate the camp to look like the 1950s, the time when many of their grandparents were kids. Read the story about Grandparent's Day. Then answer the questions.

On Grandparent's Day, it feels like we're going back in time. All the girls at Camp Summerland wear poodle skirts and blouses. The boys wear cowboy shirts and ties. We invite our grandparents to join us in hula hoop contests. After dinner, we hold a sock hop. I make sure that my grandpa's name is the first and last one on my dance card. Learning about the 1950s is fun!

Use words from the story to finish the sentences.

1. In the 1950s, many girls wore poodle skirts and blouses .

2. _____ and _____ were popular clothes for boys.

3. There were contests to see how long people could spin a _____ around their bodies.

4. At a _____, people danced in their socks.

5. _____ were used to tell who you would dance with during each song.

Batter Up!

Draw a picture, chart, or diagram to solve the story problems.
Then write the answer for each problem.

1. Kate, Marco, and Jenna are lining up for batting practice. How many different ways can they line up?

_____

J M K	K J M
J K M	M K J
K M J	M J K

2. Kate hit 16 balls on Monday, 22 balls on Wednesday, and 15 balls on Friday. How many balls did she hit in all?

_____

3. Jenna practices batting for 30 minutes a day, three days a week. How many weeks will it take her to practice for a total of 6 hours?

_____

4. Marco hit his first ball 12 feet. He hit the second ball 14 feet, and the third ball 16 feet. If he continues in this pattern, how far will he hit the tenth ball?

_____

Math Crossword

Solve the multiplication problems. Find each answer in the box. Then write it in the puzzle.

ten   sixteen   twenty   three   four

six   twelve   fourteen   nine   eighteen

1. f o u r t e e n

ACROSS

1. 7 × 2 = ___
4. 2 × 3 = ___
6. 3 × 1 = ___
7. 3 × 3 = ___
8. 4 × 5 = ___

DOWN

2. 4 × 3 = ___
3. 9 × 2 = ___
4. 4 × 4 = ___
5. 2 × 2 = ___
8. 5 × 2 = ___

Now and Then

A **verb** is a word that expresses an action. Circle the verb in each sentence. Then write the past tense of that verb on the line by adding **-d** or **-ed**.

Past Tense

1. Butter (melts) on the warm, crispy toast.   _melted_

2. Huma bakes cookies for the class.   _____

3. My dogs bark at the mail carrier.   _____

4. Horses gallop along the beach at sunset.   _____

5. The winds move the leaves across the yard.   _____

6. Shane and Bess want more pizza.   _____

7. Lin and Brett talk on the phone every day.   _____

8. Lots of people visit the new museum.   _____

9. Jason and Cris play soccer on the school team.   _____

10. Tiny ants crawl into the picnic basket.   _____

Supersonic Sluggers

The Supersonic Sluggers played eight baseball games. The graph shows the number of runs scored in each game.

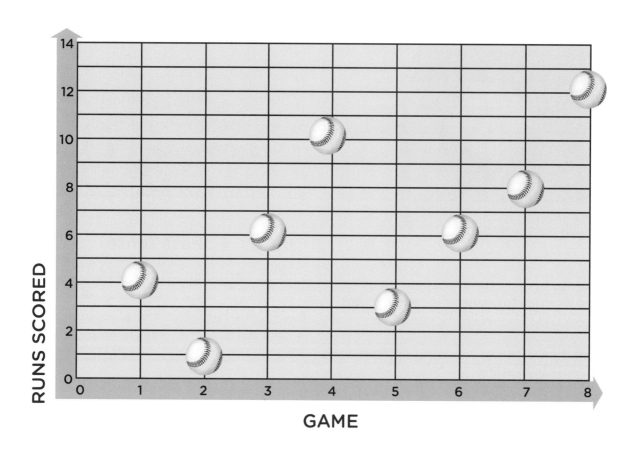

Use the graph to answer the questions.

1. How many runs did the team sore in Game 2? _____

2. In which two games did the team score the same number of runs? _____

3. What is the difference between the team's highest score and its lowest

    score? _____

4. What is the total number of runs scored in Games 5, 6, and 7? _____

Shorten It

An **abbreviation** is a shorter way of writing a word.
Abbreviations start with capital letters and end with periods.

> **Ash Street** becomes **Ash St.**
> **Monday** becomes **Mon.**
> **Doctor** becomes **Dr.**

Write the abbreviation for each underlined word.

1. I have soccer practice on <u>Tuesday</u>. Tues.

2. My coach, <u>Missus</u> Turner, likes to start on time. _____

3. We play in the park on Coral <u>Avenue</u>. _____

4. We have a game on <u>Saturday</u>. _____

5. We'll be playing the Texas Tornadoes on <u>Wednesday</u>. _____

6. Afterward, we'll go to the pizza parlor on Cactus <u>Drive</u>. _____

7. My neighbor <u>Doctor</u> Bates always buys the pizzas for my team. _____

8. The season will be over in <u>August</u>. _____

Divide It

There are ten division problems in this puzzle. Circle each problem.

HINTS:

Problems can go across or down.

A number can be used in more than one problem.

30	6	5	15	18	20
10	3	25	3	7	4
24	2	12	5	1	5
16	4	4	10	7	2
8	18	3	6	9	14

Spelling with O

Circle the correct spelling in each row. Then find the circled word that fits in each box and fill in the boxes.

1.

2.

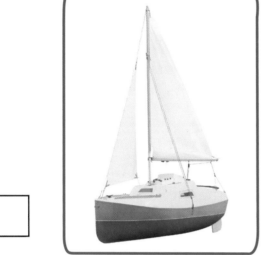

boat	boate
homme	home
clok	clock
snow	snoe
smoke	smocke
sope	soap
throw	thro
rock	roc
drov	drove
roaste	roast

3.

4.

5.

6.

7.

8.

9.

10.

Grandpa's Promise

Read the story. Then answer the questions.

Casey's sandals slapped at the bottoms of her feet as she raced along. Today was a special day. Grandpa was visiting and he had made a promise. Grandpa unlocked the gate to the swimming pool. Casey ran inside and dropped her towel on one of the plastic chairs. "Now, Grandpa? Can you show me now?"

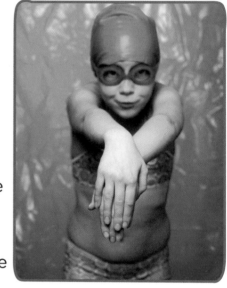

Grandpa chuckled. "Just a minute. I've got to put my glasses on first." Finally, Grandpa joined Casey by the side of the pool. "Now, put your toes right there by the edge."

Suddenly, Casey was nervous. She wondered, "What if I land on my belly? What if I crash my head against the bottom?"

Grandpa stood right beside her. "Reach your arms up over your head, like you're going to touch the sky. Then bend over like you're going to touch your toes." Grandpa watched carefully. "Ready? Go!"

Casey tipped over the side of the pool. Her fingers touched the water first, and then her body followed. She had learned the dive!

1. What had Grandpa promised Casey? _Grandpa promised to_ _teach Casey how to dive._

2. How did Casey feel at the beginning of the story? _____

_____

3. Why did Casey start to feel nervous? _____

_____

4. How do you think Casey felt at the end of the story? _____

_____

5. What word in the story means the same thing as *laughed*? _____

An Object in Motion

Follow the directions below.

Motion is what happens when something moves from where it was to a new place. **Force** is what causes an object to move. The object is pushed or pulled by force. **Speed** is how fast an object moves. **Friction** causes an object to stop moving.

Read each sentence. If the sentence is **true**, circle the bat.
If the sentence is **false**, cross out the bat.

1. When you throw a ball, you are using force to make it move.

2. It is not possible to measure the speed of a moving object.

3. Kicking a soccer ball changes the position of the ball.

4. A rolling ball can only stop if someone picks it up.

5. The harder you kick a ball, the slower it will move.

6. Friction from grass slows down a ball.

A Little Help

Machines are tools used to move objects. Machines help people use force to push or pull things. A bowling ball is a machine. When it is rolled down a bowling alley, it pushes down the bowling pins.

Circle the objects that are machines.

Making Contractions

Follow the directions below.

A **contraction** is a word formed by combining two words and leaving out some letters or sounds. For example, *can't* is a contraction of the words *can* and *not*. Write the contraction on the line for each pair of words in ( ).

1. Dad (can not) take us to the aquarium until Saturday.   _can't_

2. (We will) see lots of fish and other sea animals.   _____

3. Jess (did not) bring her camera.   _____

4. (I am) going to take some pictures for her.   _____

5. Sharks (are not) as big as whales.   _____

6. Most sharks (do not) hurt people.   _____

7. Jess and I (have not) seen real sea otters before!   _____

8. A whale (is not) a fish. It is a mammal.   _____

9. (Here is) a picture of a blue whale.   _____

10. I hope (I will) see a blue whale someday.   _____

Good Question

Why do elephants have trunks?

Solve the problems. Use subtraction to check your answers. Then use the letters next to the sums to fill in the answer to the riddle above.

1.
```
   45      98
 + 53  E - 45
 ────      ──
   98      53
```

2.
```
   26
 + 34  T - ____
 ────
```

3.
```
   75
 + 12  C - ____
 ────
```

4.
```
   18
 + 39  B - ____
 ────
```

5.
```
   69
 + 24  A - ____
 ────
```

6.
```
   35
 + 15  U - ____
 ────
```

7.
```
   47
 + 28  R - ____
 ────
```

8.
```
   29
 + 29  S - ____
 ────
```

9.
```
   61
 + 24  H - ____
 ────
```

10.
```
   17
 + 39  N - ____
 ────
```

11.
```
   63
 + 32  I - ____
 ────
```

12.
```
   55
 + 17  Y - ____
 ────
```

ANSWER

___ ___ ___ ___ ___ ___ ___   ___ ___ ___ ___   ___ ___ ___ ___ ,
57 98 87 93 50 58 98   60 85 98 72   87 93 56 60

___ ___ ___ ___ ___   ___   ___ ___ ___ ___ ___ ___ ___ ___
87 93 75 75 72   93   58 50 95 60 87 93 58 98

Counting Time

Answer the questions below.

TIME KEY

1 minute = 60 seconds   1 hour = 60 minutes   1 day = 24 hours

1 week = 7 days   1 year = 12 months

1.  Teddy ran the race in 1 minute and 12 seconds. How many seconds did it take?

_72_ seconds

2.  Pine Valley Camp lasts for 28 days. How many weeks does it last?

_____ weeks

3.  The movie was 2 hours long. How many minutes was it?

_____ minutes

4.  Earth turns on its axis every 24 hours. How many days is that?

_____ days

5.  Eric walks his dog for 1 hour each day. How many hours does he walk his dog in 2 weeks?

_____ hours

6.  Soccer season lasts 8 weeks. How many days is soccer season?

_____ days

7.  Tess spends half of the year in dance lessons. How many months is that?

_____ months

8. Corey reads for 15 minutes each day. How many hours does he read in 8 days?

_____ hours

Spelling with I

Circle the correct spelling of each word. Then find and circle the words in the word search. Words can go up, down, or diagonal.

1. ice	ise	6. littel	little
2. lim	lime	7. tiny	tiney
3. ti	tie	8. spidder	spider
4. thise	this	9. circal	circle
5. stir	stur	10. drive	driv

```
W  I  T  N  O  E  R  B  A  R
E  C  H  U  L  T  A  M  S  I
V  E  Q  C  S  T  I  R  Y  S
S  P  R  A  P  T  E  N  O  J
O  I  H  T  R  D  E  D  Y  S
C  M  Y  L  I  T  T  L  E  I
T  R  A  P  D  N  H  P  S  E
S  I  S  N  O  G  A  I  W  T
E  D  R  I  V  E  D  T  S  I
R  H  I  N  A  J  L  I  M  E
```

Swinging Subtraction

Subtract. Regroup when you need to.

1.
```
  743
- 225
```

2.
```
  321
- 221
```

3.
```
  549
- 269
```

4.
```
  936
- 777
```

5.
```
  148
-  57
```

6.
```
  250
- 109
```

7.
```
  464
- 132
```

8.
```
  659
- 269
```

9.
```
  851
- 664
```

10.
```
  638
- 229
```

11.
```
  566
- 278
```

12.
```
  886
- 499
```

Birds of a Feather

A zookeeper takes care of her zoo's birds. She made a bar graph to show the number of birds that are in her care. Look at the graph. Then answer the questions.

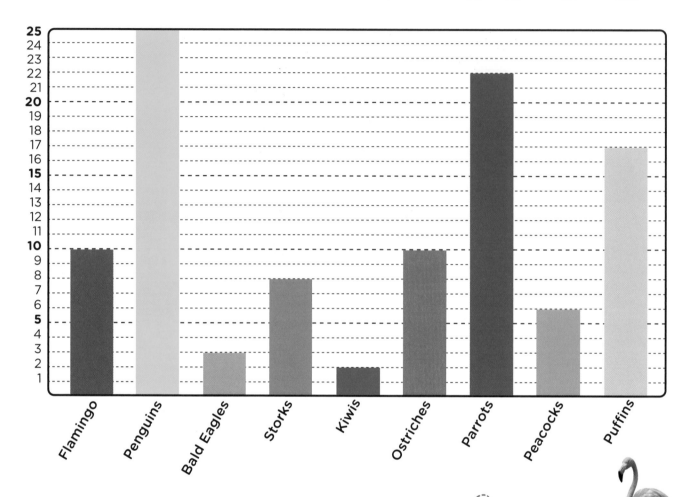

1. How many bald eagles does the zookeeper care for? ___3___
2. How many birds, all together, does the zookeeper care for? _____
3. How many more penguins are there than puffins? _____
4. How many more parrots are there than storks? _____
5. There is an equal number of which two types of birds? _____
_____

6. Which of the following is **not** found in the graph? _____
   a) the difference between the number of flamingos and the number of storks at the zoo
   b) what countries the birds are native to
   c) how many ostriches the zookeeper takes care of

Finish the Patterns

Look at each pattern. Finish each pattern by drawing it in the spaces.

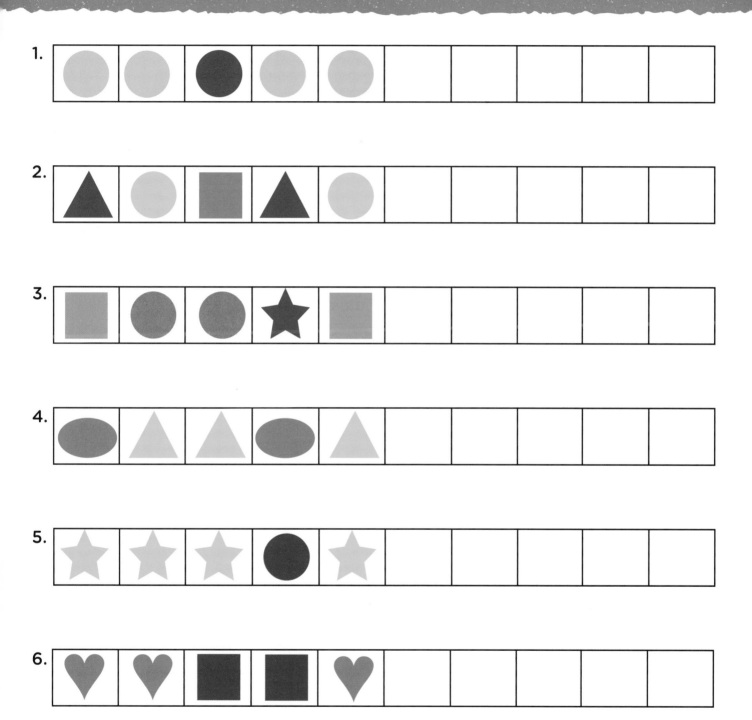

Magic Shoes

Read the story. Then answer the questions below.

Meg put on her new red tennis shoes. She tied the laces and looked at herself in the mirror. She knew it right away. These shoes were special.

Meg walked to school with her friend Chad. "I love your shoes," he told her. Meg smiled as she skipped along. It seemed as if she were walking on springs!

At softball practice, Meg almost flew around the bases. Her team was amazed. "I've never seen you run that fast!" her coach cheered. Meg scored three runs.

On her walk home, Meg stopped in her tracks. Her feet were not touching the ground! In fact, she was floating. She was flying!

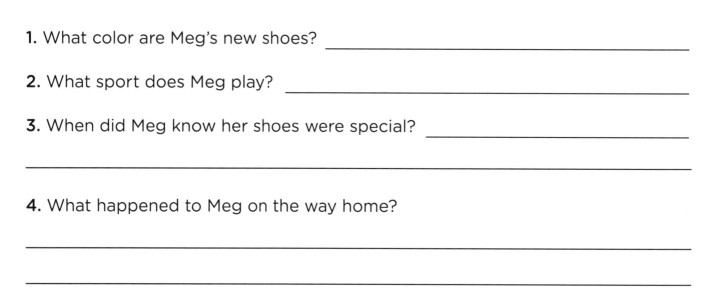

1. What color are Meg's new shoes? _____

2. What sport does Meg play? _____

3. When did Meg know her shoes were special? _____

_____

4. What happened to Meg on the way home?

_____

_____

5. On another piece of paper, write a story about what Meg did next.

A Trip to the Zoo

Sentences can be written in many different ways to make them more interesting.
They can begin with different words. They can be different lengths.
Two sentences can be combined to make one sentence.

Read each set of sentences. Rewrite them to make them more interesting.

1. My brother went to the zoo. I went with him.

   My brother and I went to the zoo.

2. We saw lions. We saw tigers. We saw bears.

   _____

   _____

3. I liked the tigers the best. My brother liked the bears better.

   _____

   _____

4. After lunch, we went to see the monkeys. After lunch, we went to see the polar bears.

   _____

   _____

5. We shopped at the gift shop before we left. I bought a T-shirt. My brother bought a T-shirt.

   _____

   _____

6. I was sad to leave the zoo. I wanted to stay longer.

   _____

   _____

Super Sentences

A sentence can end with a **period** (.), a **question mark** (?),
or an **exclamation point** (!).

A **period** is used after a statement or command. A **question mark** is used after a question. An **exclamation point** is used to show excitement. It follows an exclamation.

Use a **period**, a **question mark**, or
an **exclamation point** to finish each sentence.

1. What a great day we had _____

2. We went to the zoo and learned all about the animals _____

3. Did you know that lions walk on their tiptoes _____

4. Can you guess what a rhino uses its horns for _____

5. We looked at the giraffes _____

6. I can't believe how many amazing animals there are _____

Now practice writing your own sentences.
Write at least one statement, one question, and one exclamation point.

_____

_____

_____

_____

_____

Pen a Poem

You can use adjectives to write a poem! Look at the examples below.

Poem Form:
Noun
2 Adjectives
3 Adjectives
Rename Noun

Example:
Snow
Soft, cold
Fluffy, crunchy, fun
Ice

Write an adjective poem below. Choose an idea
from the box or use one of your own.

family	friends	seasons	pets
places	foods	sports	

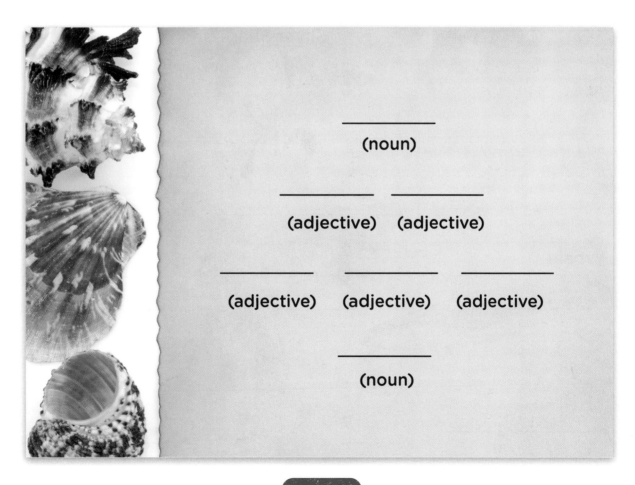

_____
(noun)

_____ _____
(adjective)   (adjective)

_____ _____ _____
(adjective)   (adjective)   (adjective)

_____
(noun)

Endangered Species

An **endangered species** of animals is one that is in danger of becoming extinct, or dying out. Many animals are endangered. Under the pictures of endangered animals, write whether the animal is a **mammal**, **bird**, or **fish**.

White-Winged Duck

_____

Giant Panda

mammal
_____

Whooping Crane

_____

Silver Shark

_____

African Elephant

Blue Whale

_____

_____

Find Your Way

Look at the zoo map. Then answer the questions.

1. In which direction would you walk to go from the elephants to the gorillas?

   northwest

2. What is directly south of the reptiles?

   _____

3. What is northwest of the giraffes?

   _____

4. Write directions telling someone how to get from the gorillas to the giraffes, and then to the elephants.

   _____

   _____

   _____

Lunch on Me!

Jeff is buying lunch for his friend. Does he have enough money? Circle **YES** or **NO**.

1.  $2.25 — YES **(circled)**   NO

2.  $1.50 — YES   NO

3.  $1.95 — YES   NO

4.  $1.80 — YES   NO

5.  $2.65 — YES   NO

Plurals, Please

A **plural** is a form of a word used to show more than one person, place, or thing.
Add **-s**, **-es**, or **-ies** to each word in ( ) to make it plural.
Write the new word on the line to finish each sentence.

1. The zoo has many kinds of __animals__ to visit.   (animal)

2. Mia wishes she could see some _____.   (zebra)

3. I want to see _____ and elephants.   (fox)

4. My _____ and I went to the zoo.   (friend)

5. The reptile house was full of big _____.   (snake)

6. We fed the monkeys _____ of bananas.   (bunch)

7. Lazy lions lay on _____ in the warm sun.   (rock)

8. We got to pet fluffy, white _____.   (bunny)

9. Panda bears peeked at us from behind _____.   (bush)

10. We even saw a tiger playing with her _____.   (baby)

The US Government

Fill in the blanks with words from the word box.

White House	Liberty Bell	Constitution
"The Star-Spangled Banner"	flag	Statue of Liberty

1. Our Founding Fathers wrote the ___Constitution___.

2. The president of the United States lives in the _____.

3. The _____ is a symbol of freedom. It cracked after arriving in the United States.

4. Francis Scott Key wrote _____ as a poem in 1814.

5. New stars were added to the _____ each time a new state joined the Union.

6. Now located in New York Harbor, the _____ was a gift from France.

Farm Food

Use the pictures to help you solve the problems.

1.

    4   +   4   +   4

3 x 4 = __12__

2.

  7 + 7 + 7 + 7 + 7

5 × 7 = _____

3.

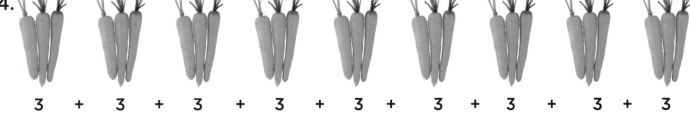

  12 + 12 + 12 + 12

4 × 12 = _____

4.

3 + 3 + 3 + 3 + 3 + 3 + 3 + 3 + 3

9 × 3 = _____

5.

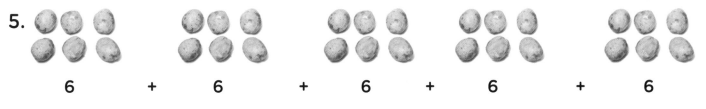

  6   +   6   +   6   +   6   +   6

5 × 6 = _____

Ice Cream Graph

Read the graph. Then answer the questions.

Favorite Ice Cream

	Chocolate	Vanilla	Mint Chip	Strawberry	Rainbow Sherbet
10					
9					X
8	X				X
7	X		X		X
6	X		X		X
5	X	X	X		X
4	X	X	X		X
3	X	X	X	X	X
2	X	X	X	X	X
1	X	X	X	X	X

1. Which ice cream was the most popular? <u>rainbow sherbet</u>

2. What was the second favorite flavor of ice cream? _____

3. How many more people liked chocolate than strawberry? _____

4. How many more people liked rainbow sherbet than vanilla? _____

5. How many people are included in the graph all together? _____

6. What is your favorite ice cream? Add your vote to the graph. Then go back and answer each question again. Did any of the answers change? If so, how?

_____

_____

Verb Search

Circle the verb in each sentence. Then write the past tense of that verb on the line.

1. Maya (goes) to the market every Saturday morning. _____went_____

2. Carla knows how to play chess. _____

3. Matt breaks track records every school year. _____

4. Peter feels the warm sand between his toes. _____

5. Jon swings the bat better than anyone else. _____

6. The coins travel to the bottom of the well. _____

7. Grandma makes my favorite cookies. _____

8. Todd throws the ball all the way down the field. _____

9. Mr. Jones feeds ducks bread in the park. _____

10. Lan draws pictures of her family. _____

Animal Pens

The farmer is building pens for his animals.
Use the word problems to help you solve the division problems.

1. There are 10 horses on the farm. Each pen can hold 5 horses. How many pens are needed?

   10 ÷ 5 = __2__

2. There are 24 pigs on the farm. Each pen can hold 8 pigs. How many pens are needed?

   24 ÷ 8 = _____

3. There are 36 cows on the farm. Each pen can hold 4 cows. How many pens are needed?

   36 ÷ 4 = _____

4. There are 48 chickens on the farm. Each pen can hold 6 chickens. How many pens are needed?

   48 ÷ 6 = _____

5. There are 27 sheep on the farm. Each pen can hold 9 sheep. How many pens are needed?

   27 ÷ 9 = _____

6. There are 33 goats on the farm. Each pen can hold 3 goats. How many pens are needed?

   33 ÷ 3 = _____

Match Up!

A **compound word** is made up of two or more words that are joined together to make a new word. Match the words to make compound words. Write the compound words on the lines.

farm	milk
barn	melon
butter	house
corn	barrow
water	bread
hay	yard
scare	stack
wheel	crow

1. _farmhouse_

2. _____

3. _____

4. _____

5. _____

6. _____

7. _____

8. _____

Fraction Fun

Write the fraction for each picture.

Example: 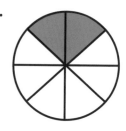 $\dfrac{3}{4}$

1.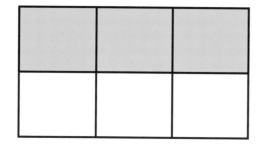

_____

2.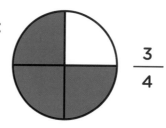

_____

3.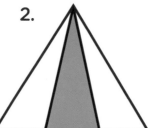

_____

4.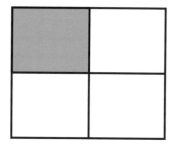

_____

5.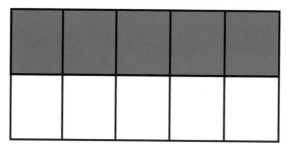

_____

6.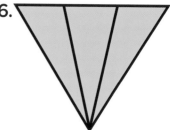

_____

7.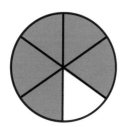

_____

8.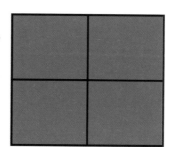

_____

9.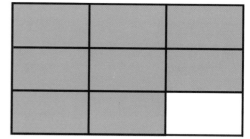

_____

Spelling with E

Circle the correct spelling in each row. Then find the circled word that fits each box and fill in the boxes.

spel	(spell)
wheel	whell
peach	peech
dere	dear
three	thrie
strete	street
clean	cleen
dead	ded
eel	eal
whent	went

1. 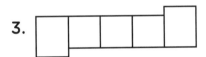 s p e l l

2.

3.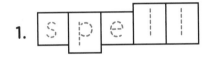

4.

5.

6.

7.

8.

9.

10.

Aunt Tonya's Farm

Read the story. Then rewrite the story using the correct capitalization.

in july, becky and jim visited aunt tonya's farm. on their first day there, they swam in sunstone creek. afterward, they hiked up butler's hill. the next day they collected eggs! aunt tonya said they could sell the eggs at the farmers' market on main street. on saturday, they helped clean the horse stalls before their riding lessons. that evening, aunt tonya took everyone on a hayride. becky and jim had a great time on the farm.

_____

_____

_____

_____

_____

_____

_____

_____

_____

_____

Did You Know?

Read the story. Then answer the questions.

Farming is a very old trade. It began thousands of years ago when people first learned how to grow crops and raise animals. Early farmers shared fields. But over time, they began to fence off their own portions of the fields. They also learned to rotate the crops that they planted. For example, if a farmer planted a field with wheat one year, the next year he might plant turnips. This helps keep the soil fresh and full of nutrients. About 200 years ago, people started to invent machines to make farming easier. Now, more food can be produced with less work. Today, about half of the world's people are farmers. Some farmers grow just enough food to feed themselves. Others grow cash crops, or food that is produced to be sold.

1. What is the story about?
   a) what life on a farm is like
   b) the history of farming
   c) a farm animal's adventures
   d) the world's most common crops

2. When did farming begin?
   a) thousands of years ago
   b) 200 years ago
   c) one year ago
   d) in the 1600s

3. Why is crop rotation a good practice?
   a) It gives the farmers more things to eat.
   b) It makes farming easier.
   c) More crops can be grown.
   d) It helps keep the soil fresh and full of nutrients.

4. About how many of the world's people are farmers?

   a) $\frac{2}{3}$ b) $\frac{1}{2}$

   c) $\frac{1}{4}$ d) $\frac{5}{6}$

5. What is a cash crop?
   a) a grove of money trees
   b) a crop that is sold
   c) a crop that is traded for other goods
   d) food that is grown just to feed the farmer

Faces of Money

Write the value for each set of coins.
Then write the number word on the lines.

1.

_____70___ ¢

s e v e n t y

2.

_____ ¢

( ) _ _ _ _

3.

_____ ¢

_ _ ( ) _ - _ _ _ _

4.

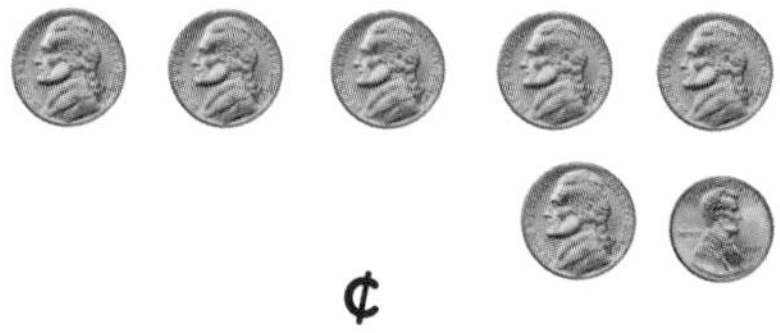

_____ ¢

_ _ _ _ _ _ - _ ( )

5.

_____ ¢

_ _ _ _ - _ _ ( )

6.

_____ ¢

_ _ _ -( )_ _

7.

_____ ¢

_( )_ _ - _ _ _

8.

_____ ¢

( )_ _ _ _ _

Write the circled letters in order to answer the question:

Which U.S. president's face is shown on the nickel?

J _ _ _ _ _ _ _ _

78

Search for Sentences

Read each paragraph. Circle the incomplete sentences.

 **1.** Azra planted a flower garden in the spring. Each day she watered the warm earth. First, tiny seedlings. Then buds began to form. Azra knew that soon pink and purple. Soon, big flowers!

 **2.** Did you know there are two kinds of elephants? Are Asian and African. Asian elephants have smaller ears. Have five front toes. African elephants are bigger. Both males and females have tusks. They only have four front toes. Like elephants? I do!

 **3.** Got a snowboard for his birthday. Over the snow really fast! Dave used to ride a skateboard. But he likes the snow better. Rides better and better. He joined a snowboarding club. Now Dave can get into some contests.

 **4.** When I grow up, I want to be an astronaut. It would be fun to fly in space. All the planets. I could count all the stars. I might even see a comet! Trip to the moon. I could gather moon rocks. To my family.

5. Now choose one of these paragraphs. Rewrite it on the lines below. Make sure all the sentences are complete!

_____

_____

_____

_____

_____

Watch Us Grow

Plants and animals need many things to grow. In the first row of boxes, draw pictures of things that plants need. In the second row, draw pictures of things that animals need.

Write a few sentences that tell about
the things that plants and animals need.

_____

_____

_____

_____

_____

_____

Sports Stories

Read each story. Write the sport described
on the line. Hint: Not all sports will be used.

hiking	baseball	tennis
swimming	biking	boating	skiing

1. Dina put on her suit. She grabbed a towel and walked to the beach. Before going in, she puts on lots of sunscreen. She did not want to get a sunburn.

   <u>swimming</u>

2. Trey put on his boots. He put a snack and a bottle of water in his pack. Then he looked at his map. Trey grabbed his walking stick and started up the trail.

   _____

3. Luke put on his cap and went outside. He carried his mitt and bat under his arm. He would put his cleats on at the field. It was a perfect day for a game!

   _____

4. "Put on your life jacket," Mom said. Krista put it on. Then they pushed off from the dock. Mom and Krista put their oars in the water and started to row.

   _____

5. Carlos pedaled as fast as he could. His legs were pumping. His hands gripped the handlebars. Wind whistled by his helmet. He made it to the top of the hill!

   _____

Business as Usual

Farms are businesses. They provide food that people need.
Choose the answer for each question below.

1. John and Maya have a business. They clean out the animal pens at farms in their town. Which of these statements is true about their business?
   a) John and Maya make things to sell.
   b) John and Maya sell things for other people.
   c) John and Maya provide a service.

2. Which of the following is the most likely to cause the cost of corn to go up?
   a) A storm damages many crops.
   b) Farm workers earn less money.
   c) The price of tomatoes goes down.

3. Brenda says she will repair one of Tom's fences if he will paint her barn. Which of these statements is true about Brenda and Tom?
   a) They will not get money for the work they do for each other.
   b) Brenda will be paid for her work.
   c) Tom will sell Brenda's barn.

4. For lunch, Brianna is having a peanut butter sandwich, an apple, a cookie, and milk. Which statement is probably true?
   a) Brianna's family owns a farm and made all of the items in her lunch.
   b) Brianna's family went to a farm and traded things for the items in her lunch.
   c) The items in Brianna's lunch were bought at a store. The store bought the items from many different businesses.

5. A dairy farm is the largest business in a small town. Which statement is probably true?
   a) The farm provides many jobs for the people in the town.
   b) The farm sells fruits and vegetables to the people in the town.
   c) The farm pays for the people's houses.

Skipping up the Mountain

Start at the bottom of each mountain. Skip count your way to the top.

1. Count by 50

8,500
8,450
8,400
8,350
8,300
8,250
8,200
8,150

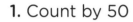

2. Count by 100

4,140
_____
_____
_____
_____
_____
_____
3,440

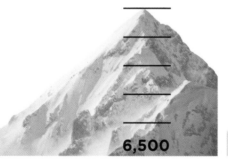

3. Count by 30

585
_____
_____
_____
_____
_____
_____
375

4. Count by 250

2,925
_____
_____
_____
_____
_____
1,175

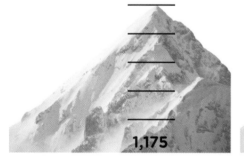

5. Count by 500

10,000
_____
_____
_____
_____
_____
6,500

6. Count by 1,000

9,372
_____
_____
_____
_____
_____
2,372

Train Time

Read the train schedule. Then answer the questions.

Train	To	Departs	Arrives
2	Vast Valley	10:00 AM	12:30 PM
4	Wild Woods	11:15 AM	2:15 PM
6	Teeny Town	12:45 PM	3:30 PM
8	Snow City	2:30 PM	4:45 PM
10	Cat's Creek	5:00 PM	9:15 PM

1. Which train has the shortest trip? Train 8

2. Which train has the longest trip? _____

3. How long is the trip to Teeny Town? _____

4. How much longer is the trip to Wild Woods than to Vast Valley?

_____

5. How much longer is the trip to Cat's Creek than to Snow City?

_____

6. The train to Vast Valley is $1\frac{1}{2}$ hours late. What time will it arrive?

_____

Name the Sentence

Answer the questions below.

A **telling** sentence makes a statement. It ends with a period (.). A **command** tells someone to do something. It ends with a period (.). An **asking** sentence asks a question. It ends with a question mark (**?**). An **exclamation** shows strong feeling. It ends with an exclamation point (**!**).

Add the correct ending punctuation to each sentence. Then write **T** for **telling**, **C** for **command**, **A** for **asking**, and **E** for **exclamation**.

1. Did you see that shooting star?   A

2. Wow, there are many, many stars in the sky   _____

3. Eight planets are in our solar system   _____

4. Would you like to go to the moon   _____

5. Bring moon rocks back from your trip   _____

6. Get ready to ride the fast rocket   _____

7. Mars is called the red planet   _____

8. Is the sun a planet or a star   _____

9. Never look at the sun   _____

10. How many rings are around Saturn   _____

Tent Time

Write the number shown on each tent in expanded form.

1. 1,265

1,000 + 200 + 60 + 5

2. 6,732

_____ + _____ + _____ + _____

3. 8,388

_____ + _____ + _____ + _____

4. 3,954

_____ + _____ + _____ + _____

5. 2,542

_____ + _____ + _____ + _____

6. 4,320

_____ + _____ + _____ + _____

7. 5,555

_____ + _____ + _____ + _____

8. 7,021

_____ + _____ + _____ + _____

The Main Idea

The main idea tells what a paragraph is mostly about.
Read each paragraph. Then circle the main idea.

1. Fall is the best time of year. The air is crisp and cool. I jump in piles of colorful leaves. Mom bakes apple pie. But best of all, I get to go back to school and see my friends.
   a) Fall weather is cold.
   b) Fall is a great season.
   c) I like leaves.

2. Some people think cats can't be trained. This is not true. It's actually very easy! First, be calm and gentle. Repeat tricks over and over again. Give your cat lots of treats as a reward. Soon your kitty will do anything you want.
   a) Cats love treats.
   b) Cats can't do tricks.
   c) You can train your cat.

3. Have you ever been to the circus? Clowns make you laugh. People ride elephants. Acrobats leap through the air. There's so much to see and do. I can't wait to go to the circus!
   a) Clowns are funny.
   b) The circus is fun.
   c) There are elephants at the circus.

4. Be safe when you ride your bike. Wear a helmet to protect your head. Look both ways before crossing the street. Make a signal before turning. Always look out for cars. Drivers may not see you. Have fun, but be safe.
   a) Bike safety is important.
   b) Drivers never see bikers.
   c) Bike helmets are cool.

What's the Big Idea?

The **main idea** of a story is what the story is mostly about.
Read the paragraph below, then answer questions about the main idea.

The Landers family couldn't wait to go camping. Four days in the fresh mountain air were just what they needed. Kurt planned on hiking to Mirror Lake. Amelia hoped to go on a horseback ride. Mr. Landers wanted to go bird-watching. Mrs. Landers brought her sketch pad so that she could draw pictures of the delicate meadow flowers. It was going to be a vacation that the whole family would enjoy.

What is the main idea of the paragraph?

_____

_____

_____

Read each group of ideas. Then write a main idea for each group.

| build a campfire | tell stories |
| toast marshmallows | look at the stars |

The main idea is

_____

_____

| packing a suitcase | making campground reservations |
| toasting marshmallows | looking at the stars |

The main idea is

_____

_____

| mountain biking | swimming |
| hiking | horseback riding |

The main idea is

_____

_____

Camp Cursive

Trace the cursive letters.

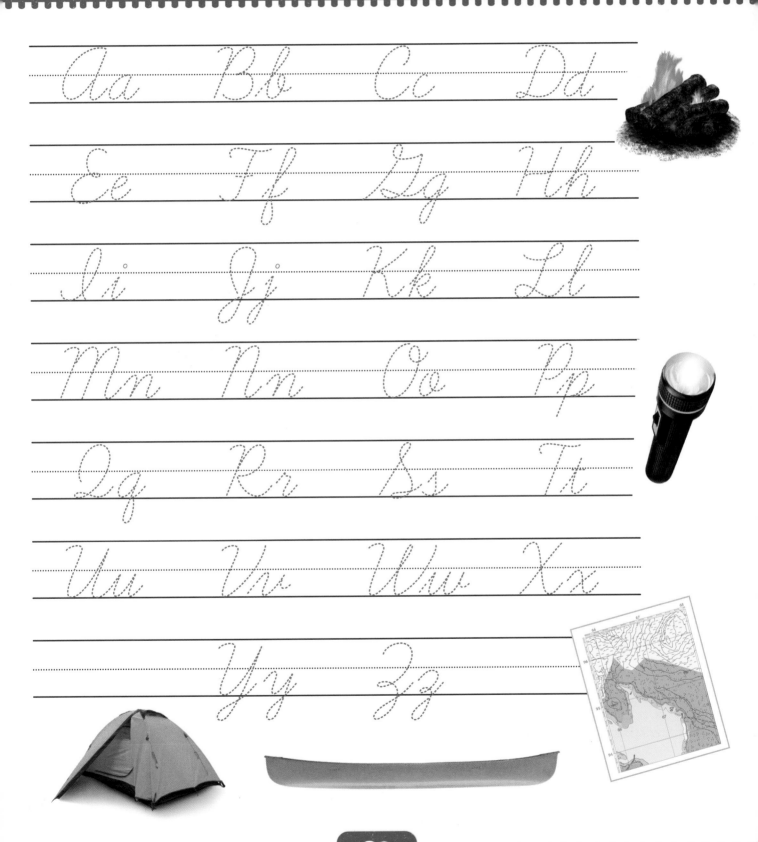

Aa   Bb   Cc   Dd

Ee   Ff   Gg   Hh

Ii   Jj   Kk   Ll

Mm   Nn   Oo   Pp

Qq   Rr   Ss   Tt

Uu   Vv   Ww   Xx

Yy   Zz

Animal Riddles

Write the answer to each problem in the box. Use the Answer Key to find the letter that matches each answer. Write the letters on the lines below to answer the riddles.

Answer Key

4	7	0	11	2	5	8	1	9	3	10	12	6
A	K	G	S	D	P	U	O	H	R	C	Q	E

What happens when a duck flies upside down?

72 ÷ 8	66 ÷ 11
9	

 H
___   ___

144 ÷ 12	56 ÷ 7	16 ÷ 4	50 ÷ 5	21 ÷ 3	99 ÷ 9

___   ___   ___   ___   ___   ___

64 ÷ 8	60 ÷ 12

___   ___

Spelling with U

Circle the correct spelling of each word. Then find and circle the words in the word search. Words can go up, down, or diagonal.

1. turtel	(turtle)	6. tru	true
2. cube	cueb	7. fur	furr
3. birst	burst	8. funny	funey
4. push	pushe	9. fuel	fule
5. pupel	pupil	10. bluw	blue

W T R U T B H O A Y

I P U P I L E S R P

V A C R U A T L T U

B U R S T O R E W S

U G H O R L U L P H

M L K M Y N E S L I

A K B N O U C H U N

U O N L F E A T O R

K U L C U B E S U S

F I H U P E J F U E

Creative Constellations

Constellations are groups of stars that together form a picture in the sky. Here are some star maps that show three constellations that can be seen from North America in the summer months.

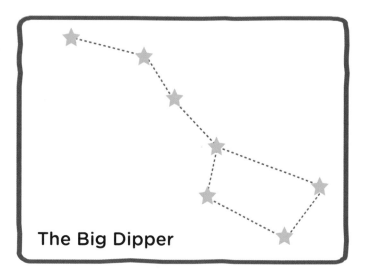

The Big Dipper

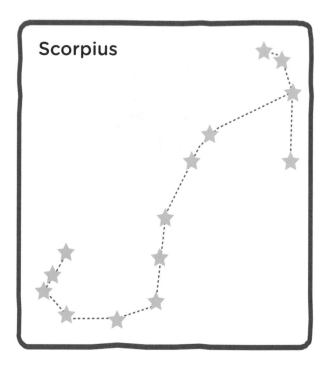

Scorpius

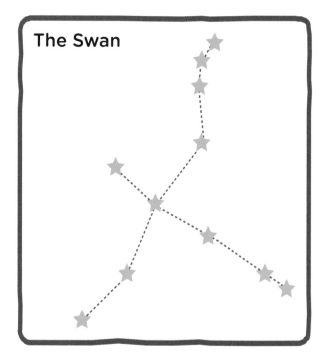

The Swan

How do you think these constellations got their names?

_____

_____

_____

_____

_____

Home, Sweet Home

Read the story. Then answer the questions.

Before the Europeans came to North America, there were
five main cultural groups of Native Americans. Each group
had its own way of life and lived in its
own type of home. Native Americans used the natural
resources around them to build their homes.

   The Northwest Indians lived in wooden lodges.
Each lodge was large enough for several families to live
together. The lodges were built from wood and bark.
Outside each lodge, there was a totem pole.
   The California-Intermountain Indians lived in wickiups.
These were circular homes made from arched poles and covered with brush.
   The Southwest Indians lived in pueblos. Pueblos were apartment-style buildings
made from adobe and clay. Many families lived together in each apartment and
new rooms were added as the families grew.
   The Plains Indians used buffalo skins to make tepees. The skins were attached
to long wooden poles and decorated with paints. Tepees could be put up and
taken down quickly so that the people could follow the buffalo.
   The Eastern Woodland Indians lived in longhouses. These homes were similar to
the Northwest Indian homes. They were built from wooden frames and covered in
bark. Several families lived together in each home.

1. Why did Native Americans live in different kinds of homes? _____

_____

2. Which two groups lived in homes that were similar to each other? What kind of
   environment do you think these groups lived in? _____

_____

3. Which group of Native Americans probably moved around the most? How
   would their type of homes help them to do this? _____

_____

Lots of Legs

Read the questions. Write your answer on the lines.

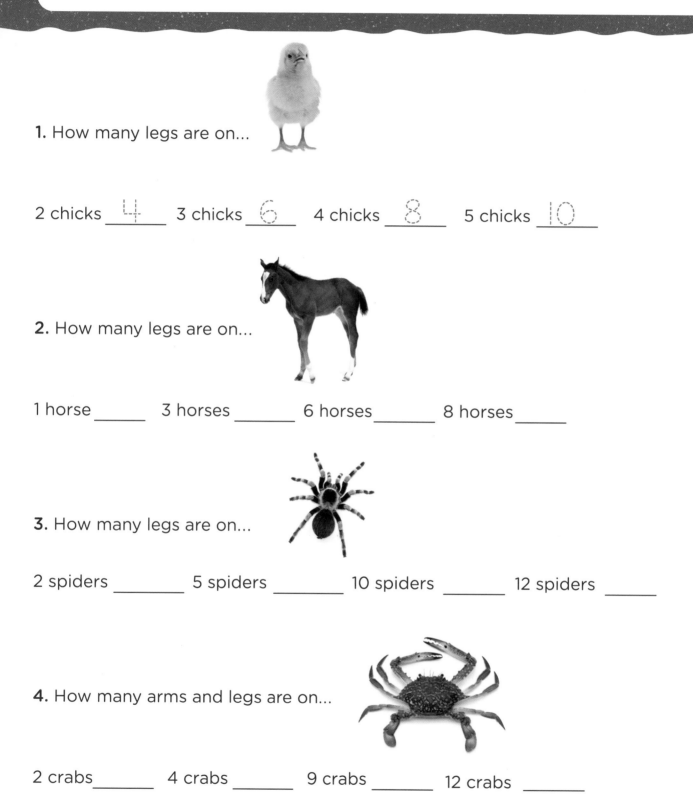

1. How many legs are on...

2 chicks __4__   3 chicks __6__   4 chicks __8__   5 chicks __10__

2. How many legs are on...

1 horse _____   3 horses _____   6 horses _____   8 horses _____

3. How many legs are on...

2 spiders _____   5 spiders _____   10 spiders _____   12 spiders _____

4. How many arms and legs are on...

2 crabs _____   4 crabs _____   9 crabs _____   12 crabs _____

What Happened Next?

Read each paragraph. Then write what happened next on the lines.

1. Big, puffy gray clouds filled the sky. The wind began to blow. As Sam walked home from school, she felt droplets on her face. Leaves blew around her feet in circles. Sam realized she had left her umbrella at home. What happened next?

_____

_____

_____

2. Ethan was a good pitcher. He and his dad practiced every day after school. The big game was coming up fast. Ethan knew the more he practiced, the better he would be. On the day of the game, Ethan was nervous. He sat on the bench, his heart pounding. What happened next?

_____

_____

_____

3. The earth shook. The huge mountain rumbled as smoked poured from its top. For days, the mountain spoke. It didn't speak softly. It roared! But on this day, it roared louder. Smoke and ash filled the sky. What happened next?

_____

_____

_____

Faces in the Mountain

Mount Rushmore is in the Black Hills of South Dakota. It is a monument to honor George Washington, Thomas Jefferson, Theodore Roosevelt, and Abraham Lincoln. These men were American presidents.

If you were hired to design a sculpture that would honor four American heroes, whom would you choose to feature in your sculpture? Draw a picture of your design here.

Write about why you selected these people for your sculpture.

_____

_____

_____

_____

_____

Beach Ball Bonanza

Multiply the numbers in the beach balls.

1. 
$2 \times 6 =$
_____

2. 
$3 \times 8 =$
_____

3. 
$5 \times 5 =$
_____

4. 
$9 \times 2 =$
_____

5. 
$4 \times 1 =$
_____

6. 
$8 \times 5 =$
_____

7. 
$6 \times 7 =$
_____

8. 
$5 \times 2 =$
_____

9. 
$3 \times 7 =$
_____

10. 
$4 \times 4 =$
_____

11. 
$8 \times 1 =$
_____

12. 
$5 \times 9 =$
_____

Write It Out

Write out each number in thousands, hundreds, tens, and ones.

Example: 3,551 = 3,000 + 500 + 50 + 1

1. 8,295

_____ = _____ + _____ + _____ + _____

2. 1,047

_____ = _____ + _____ + _____ + _____

3. 9,962

_____ = _____ + _____ + _____ + _____

4. 6,813

_____ = _____ + _____ + _____ + _____

5. Write as many 3-digit numbers as you can using: 5, 3, 9.

_____   _____   _____

_____   _____   _____

Circle the smallest number. Cross out the largest number.

6. Write as many 3-digit numbers as you can using: 6, 8, 2.

_____   _____   _____

_____   _____   _____

Circle the smallest number. Cross out the largest number.

Interesting Words

Good writing has interesting words. There is usually more than one way to describe something! Read the words in the box.

sticky	irritated	glad	asked	thrilled	angry	gooey	cranky
roared	rough	joyful	groaned	cross	prickly	cried	cheerful

- Find 4 words that mean **happy**.
- Find 4 words that mean **mad**.
- Find 4 words that mean **said**.
- Find 4 words that describe how something **feels** when you touch it.

Write each group of words in the word puzzles

1. Happy

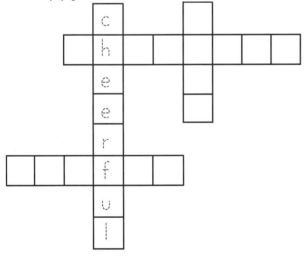

2. Mad

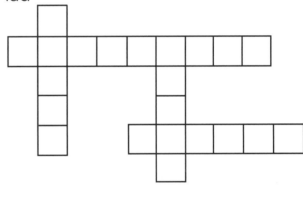

3. Said

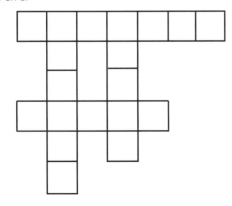

4. Feels

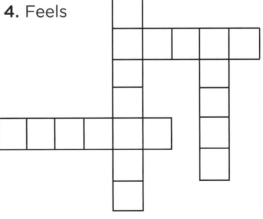

Sharing Shells

Circle the shells to solve the problems. Write the answers.

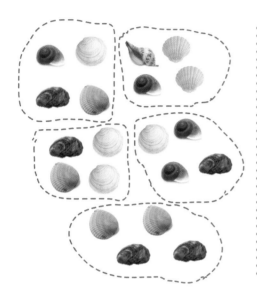  

1. 20 ÷ 4 = __5__

2. 12 ÷ 3 = ____

3. 18 ÷ 6 = ____

Solve the problems.

4. 20 ÷ 5 = ____

5. 15 ÷ 3 = ____

6. 10 ÷ 2 = ____

7. 40 ÷ 4 = ____

8. 9 ÷ 3 = ____

9. 12 ÷ 4 = ____

10. 16 ÷ 4 = ____

11. 25 ÷ 5 = ____

12. 18 ÷ 6 = ____

In Other Words

A **thesaurus** gives synonyms for words. Sometimes it also gives antonyms.

Look at the entries below. Underline the synonyms. Circle the antonyms.

1. **happy**   glad, cheerful, sad, gloomy, joyous, unhappy, joyful, merry
2. **hot**   chilly, cold, fiery, frosty, flaming, scorching, frozen, sweaty
3. **sparkling**   glistening, dark, glittery, glimmering, dim, gloomy, shimmering, murky

happy	glad	cheerful	sad	gloomy
joyous	unhappy	joyful	merry	hot
fiery	flaming	scorching	sweaty	chilly
cold	frosty	frozen	sparkling	glistening
glittery	glimmering	shimmering	dark	dim
gloomy	murky			

Choose synonyms from the box to rewrite these sentences.

4. It was a hot day at the beach. I went for a swim in the sparkling water.

_____

_____

5. Choose antonyms to rewrite the sentences.

_____

_____

A thesaurus is organized like a dictionary. It lists words alphabetically. Guide words at the top of the page tell the first and the last words on each page.

Read the sets of guide words. Circle the words that would go on the same page.

6. **beach/beneath** before, beyond, blast
7. **cloudy/comment** common, cold, clean
8. **ocean/open** odor, operate, ornament

Our Pets

This is a **pie chart**. It shows the number of people who have different kinds of pets. Read the chart. Then answer the questions.

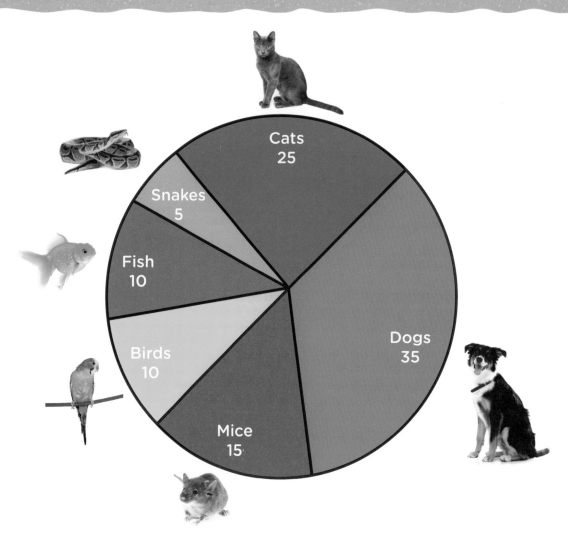

1. How many people have dogs? _____

2. How many people have cats? _____

3. How many more people have dogs than fish? _____

4. How many more people have mice than snakes? _____

5. How many people do not have cats? _____

6. How many people have pets altogether? _____

Surprise in the Box

Think of an object to put in each box. Write five adjectives to describe it in the box. Then write the name of the object.

1.

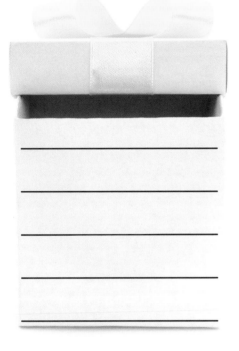

It is a _____ !

2.

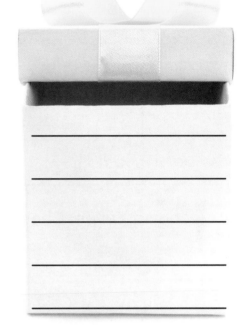

It is a _____ !

3.

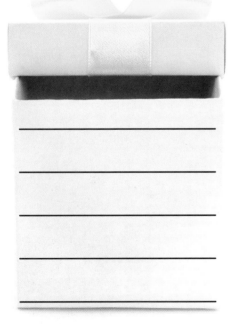

It is a _____ !

4.

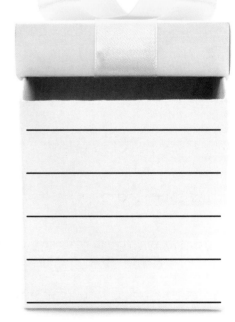

It is a _____ !

The Endings

A **suffix** is a small group of letters added to the end of a word.
A suffix changes the meaning of the word.

Suffix	Meaning	Example
-er and -or	one who _____	farm + er = farmer
-ful	full of _____	thought + ful = thoughtful
-less	without _____	care + less = careless

Rewrite each sentence. Change the underlined words to words that have suffixes of **-er, -or, -ful**, or **-less**.

1. The underline{person swimming} caught the lifeguard's attention.

   The swimmer caught the lifeguard's attention.

2. He was underline{without a thought} and had drifted out to deep water.

   _____

3. A underline{man sailing} was underline{full of care} when he tossed the life jacket.

   _____

4. "I am underline{full of thanks} that you rescued me," he said.

   _____

5. The lifeguard told him that he should hire a underline{person who teaches swimming}.

   _____

6. "You have been so underline{full of help}," said the swimmer.

   _____

   _____

Mixed-Up Picnic

There's a picnic at the beach, but things have gotten all mixed up!
Help fix the picnic by writing instructions for making a sandwich.
Use all the words in the word box.

first	second	then
next	last	

_____

_____

_____

_____

_____

_____

Liquid Measures

Use the Measuring Key to solve the problems. Then write your answer in the crossword puzzle. Use number words.

Measuring Key

3 teaspoons (tsp) = 1 tablespoon (Tbsp)

2 Tbsp = 1 ounce

8 ounces = 1 cup

2 cups = 1 pint

2 pints = 1 quart

4 quarts = 1 gallon

1. S I X T E E N

2.

3.

4.

5.

6.

7.

8.

9.

10.

ACROSS

2. $\frac{1}{2}$ gallon = _____ cups

4. 12 pints = _____ quarts

5. 6 cups = _____ pints

7. 33 tsp = _____ Tbsp

9. 1 quart = _____ ounces

DOWN

1. 2 cups = _____ ounces

3. 3 Tbsp = _____ tsp

6. 10 cups = _____ ounces

8. 1 quart = _____ cups

10. 32 Tbsp = _____ cups

Dear Friend...

Write a letter to a friend or a family member. Tell this person about something special you are doing this summer. Are you taking a special trip? Are you taking lessons? Are you visiting a relative?

Remember to follow these rules:
- Use interesting words.
- Use correct punctuation.
- Use complete sentences.

_____
(Date)

Dear _____,

_____

_____

_____

_____

_____

_____

_____

_____

Your friend,

_____

Ride the Waves

Read the story. Then answer the questions.

The seashore is where the ocean meets the land. At high tide, ocean water covers much of the land at the shore. At low tide, the water rolls back into the ocean, and we see the sloping shore. Tides change from day to day throughout the month. They are created by the force of gravity between the moon, Earth, and the sun. When the moon, Earth, and the sun are in line with one another, there will be spring tides. Spring tides come in very high and then go back out to sea very far. They occur every 14 to 15 days, during a new moon or a full moon. When the moon, Earth, and the sun are at right angles to one another, neap tides occur. During neap tides, there is little difference between the heights of high tide and low tide. Neap tides form during the first and last quarters of the moon's cycle.

1. What happens to the shore during high tide?
   Ocean water covers much of the land at the shore.

2. What creates the tides?
   _____

3. Why are the tides different from day to day?
   _____

4. What are spring tides? When do they occur?
   _____

5. During neap tides, how are the moon, Earth, and the sun aligned with each other?
   _____

Ocean Predators

Read the story. Then solve the puzzle.

When people think of **predators**, they often think of large, fierce animals that hunt and capture other animals. While this is accurate, a predator is any animal that kills its food. The animals that are hunted and killed are called **prey**. In the ocean, there are strong, massive predators that swim in the open water, as well as smaller predators that bury themselves in the sand or hide in caves. Ocean

predators use many different methods to hunt. Elephant seals, great white sharks, and barracudas use their speed and strength to overpower other animals. Others, like stonefish and spotted groupers, use camouflage to hide themselves until their prey swims close enough to be captured. An anglerfish lures its prey with a long, thin fin that glows and wiggles. Once a fish is attracted to the lure, the anglerfish opens its mouth and sucks in its victim. Some ocean animals, such as killer whales and bluefish, hunt in groups. Working together, these predators confuse their prey, cut off their escape routes, and often drive them to exhaustion. A predator's senses are perhaps its most important set of hunting tools. Without the ability to locate food using sight, sound, or smell, the predator would not have the ability to feed itself.

Down
1. Stonefish method for capturing prey
2. Hunted animals
4. Anglerfish uses its fin as this

Across
2. Hunter
3. Type of fish that hunts in groups
5. Type of fish that uses speed and strength to hunt
6. Important hunting tools

Perimeter Puzzlers

Perimeter is the distance all the way around the edge of an object.

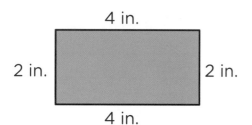

4 in.

2 in.   2 in.

4 in.

P = 2 in. + 2 in. + 4 in. + 4 in. = 12 in.

Write the perimeter of each shape.

1.

3 in.

1 in.   1 in.

3 in.

P = _____

2.

5 in.

5 in.   5 in.

5 in.

P = _____

3.

6 in.   6 in.

2 in.

P = _____

4.

2 cm   2 cm

2 cm   2 cm

2 cm

P = _____

5.

8 in.

4 in.   4 in.

8 in.

P = _____

6.

2 cm

5 cm   6 cm

5 cm

P = _____

Details, Details!

Every paragraph has a main idea. The main idea is supported by **details**. These details further describe and develop the main idea.

Underline the supporting details in each paragraph.

1. I took my first train ride today. I sat by the window so I could watch the world go by. We crossed over a river. When we passed through the train stations, people waved at me! I waved back with a big smile on my face. What a great trip!

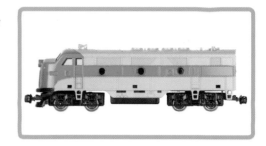

2. Rainbows form when water and light come together. The water can come from anywhere. It can be rain. It can be spray from a garden hose. It can come from a water fountain. The water source is not important.

3. Now, write your own main idea and supporting details. Write your main idea in the center circle. Write details about that idea in the circles around it.

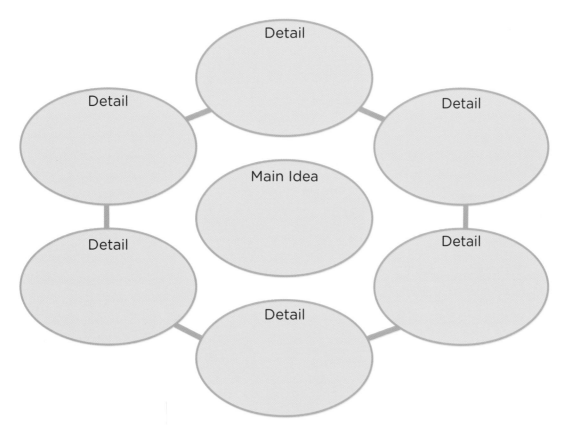

Place-Value Puzzles

Read each puzzle. Write the number.

1. My ones digit is 3. My tens digit is 2 less than my ones digit. My hundreds digit is 3 times larger than my tens digit. My thousands digit is 1 more than my hundreds digit.

What's my number? _4,313_

2. My ones digit is 3. My tens digit is 4 more than my ones digit. My hundreds digit is 2 less than my tens digit. My thousands digit is 1 more than my hundreds digit. My ten-thousands digit is half of my thousands digit.

What's my number? _____

3. My hundreds digit is 2. My tens digit is half of my hundreds digit. My thousands digit is 4 times larger than my tens digit. My ones digit is double my thousands digit. My ten-thousands digit is 6 more than my hundreds digit.

What's my number? _____

4. My thousands digit is 4. My ten-thousands digit is 5 more than my thousands digit. My hundreds digit is 2 less than my thousands digit. My tens digit is 4 less than my thousands digit. My ones digit is less than my thousands digit, but greater than my hundreds digit.

What's my number? _____

Follow each set of directions.

5. Use the digits **6, 9, 0, 2**. Write the smallest 4-digit number. _____

6. Use the digits **1, 3, 5, 7**. Write the greatest 4-digit number. _____

Brain Stumpers

Read the clues to solve each problem.

1. How many marbles are in the bag?
   - There are more than 20 and less than 30.
   - You can divide the marbles equally into groups of 3.
   - If you divide the marbles into groups of 5, 1 will be left over.

There are __21__ marbles in the bag.

2. Keri, Ana, Ahmad, and Juan were all born in the same year. Who is the oldest? Write 1, 2, 3, 4 to put the children in older, oldest to youngest.
   - Juan's birthday is between Ahmad's and Keri's.
   - Ana has the first birthday in the group.
   - Keri is younger than Ahmad.

Keri _____ Ana _____ Ahmad _____ Juan _____

3. How many coins are in the jar?
   - There are more than 30 and less than 50.
   - You can divide the coins equally into groups of 6.
   - If you divide the coins into groups of 5, 3 will be left over.

There _____ are coins in the jar.

Read All About It!

Newspaper articles tell about events in the community. Look at a newspaper. Read the headlines. They grab your attention! Articles also answer these questions:

Who? What? When? Where? How?

Write an article about an event in your family or neighborhood. Make sure to answer the questions who, what, when, where, and how. Remember to write a great headline!

Draw a picture

Packing for the Picnic

Unit cost is the price for a single item. To find the unit cost, divide the total price by the number of items. Determine the unit cost for each item below.

Forks 8 per box $3.20	**Paper Plates** bag of 50 $5.00	**Sodas** 6-pack $3.60	**Juice Boxes** 12-pack $4.80
Fried Chicken 10-piece bucket $3.20	**Dinner Rolls** 15 count $4.50	**Oranges** 8 per bag $3.60	**Cupcakes** box of 12 $4.80

1.

2.

3.

4.

The cost of 8 forks is $3.20.

$$8\overline{)3.20} = .40$$

The cost of one fork is $0.40

5.

6.

7.

8.

Yum! Yum!

Help the bear find its way to the picnic. Add or subtract the fractions.
Put each fraction in lowest terms. Then color
the boxes that have an answer with odd numerators.

$$\frac{5}{8} + \frac{2}{8} = \frac{7}{8}$$

$$\frac{1}{4} + \frac{2}{4} =$$

$$\frac{2}{6} + \frac{2}{6} =$$

$$\frac{8}{12} + \frac{2}{12} =$$

$$\frac{3}{16} - \frac{1}{16} =$$

$$\frac{3}{5} + \frac{1}{5} =$$

$$\frac{7}{10} + \frac{2}{10} =$$

$$\frac{11}{12} + \frac{3}{12} =$$

$$\frac{7}{8} - \frac{1}{8} =$$

$$\frac{1}{4} + \frac{2}{4} =$$

$$\frac{3}{8} + \frac{4}{8} =$$

$$\frac{8}{10} - \frac{1}{10} =$$

$$\frac{6}{7} - \frac{2}{7} =$$

$$\frac{8}{12} - \frac{2}{12} =$$

$$\frac{2}{6} + \frac{3}{6} =$$

$$\frac{10}{10} - \frac{2}{10} =$$

$$\frac{5}{6} - \frac{3}{6} =$$

$$\frac{1}{4} + \frac{3}{4} =$$

$$\frac{1}{3} + \frac{1}{3} =$$

$$\frac{5}{9} + \frac{2}{9} =$$

$$\frac{4}{8} - \frac{1}{8} =$$

$$\frac{7}{11} - \frac{3}{11} =$$

$$\frac{8}{9} - \frac{4}{9} =$$

$$\frac{3}{12} + \frac{3}{12} =$$

$$\frac{4}{11} - \frac{2}{11} =$$

$$\frac{1}{5} + \frac{2}{5} =$$

Changing Words

A **prefix** is a word part added to the front of a base word.
A prefix changes the meaning of that word.

Read the meanings of the prefixes. Then read the definitions below. Make a new word to match each definition by adding a prefix. Then write a brand-new word with the same prefix.

Prefixes

re-	again	**un-**	not
bi-	two	**over-**	too much
under-	below	**non-**	not
mis-	wrong	**multi-**	many, much

New Word

1. Write again   _____re_ write   _rewind_____

2. Cycle with two wheels   _____ cycle   _____

3. Not happy   _____ happy   _____

4. Below ground   _____ ground   _____

5. Pay too much   _____ paid   _____

6. Not able   _____ able   _____

7. Many colored   _____ colored   _____

8. Count wrong   _____ count   _____

9. Does not stop   _____ stop   _____

10. Heat again   _____ heat   _____

Write two sentences. Use one of your new words in each sentence.

11. _____

12. _____

Soundalikes

Homophones are words that sound alike, but they are spelled differently and have different meanings.

Use the pairs of homophones to complete the sentences.

bare / bear	fir / fur	close / clothes
chews / choose	ate / eight	creek / creak

1. Elena dipped her _bare_ feet into the cool _creek_ .

2. Which _____ would you _____ to wear?

3. The _____ scratched at its _____ .

4. We _____ near the _____ tree.

5. When I _____ the lid to the picnic basket, I hear it _____ .

6. My terrier _____ on _____ bones a day.

Homographs are words that look and sound alike but have different meanings. Each word below has more than one meaning. Draw a picture to show two of the word's meanings.

bat		bill		palm	

Personality Plus

Authors use descriptions, dialogue, and actions to make their characters come to life. Read the passages below. Write a description of each character's personality based on what you read.

1. Noah looked through his binoculars and found the robin's nest. The eggs had finally hatched, and he could hear the tiny birds inside. He looked around for the parent birds but did not see them anywhere. "Don't worry," he whispered to the babies. "I'll make sure you're safe until they get back."

   _____

   _____

2. Daniel raced through the park. He couldn't believe he was late again. He hoped his coach wouldn't bench him. Today's game was for the championship, and Daniel just had to play. Suddenly, he stopped dead in his tracks. "Holy cow!" he said. "I left my bat at home."

   _____

   _____

3. Alicia peeked into the box of cookies. She counted two, four, six, eight. "There's enough for two each," she told her brother and sister. When they weren't looking, Alicia slipped the extra two cookies in her pocket.

   _____

   _____

4. The blistering sun seared Moira's skin. She dabbed at her forehead with the edge of her shirtsleeve. She looked toward the top of the hill and took a gulp of water. "I'm almost there," she said to herself. "I'm not giving up until I make it."

   _____

   _____

Making Comparisons

Follow the directions below.

Adjectives that compare two things usually end in **-er**.
Example: Chloe is <u>taller</u> than Zane.

Adjectives that compare more than two things usually end in **-est**.
Example: Zane is the <u>smartest</u> boy in class.

Circle the adjective that best completes each sentence.

1. Meg is the (sweeter, sweetest) girl in second grade.

2. Whales are the (bigger, biggest) animals in the sea.

3. My speech is 10 minutes (longer, longest) than yours.

4. Mount Everest is the (taller, tallest) mountain in the world.

5. Nick is a (stronger, strongest) ball player than Jared.

6. Cheetahs can run (faster, fastest) than lions.

7. The sun seems (brighter, brightest) today than yesterday.

8. My grandpa is the (funnier, funniest) man I know.

9. I think football is (harder, hardest) than soccer.

10. February is the (shorter, shortest) month of the year.

Use these adjectives to write sentences that compare.

11. cold _____

12. nice _____

How Does Your Garden Grow?

Read the story. Then look at the pictures below. Write a sentence for each one that describes how the plant most likely reproduces.

Plants, like animals, can reproduce. This means that plants can make new plants like themselves. Different plants reproduce in different ways. Flowering plants use pollen to reproduce. The pollen is transferred from one flower to another, either by wind or by insects. Large amounts of pollen are produced to make sure that some will be caught by other flowers. Many plants reproduce by growing buds that drop off the plant and start new lives of their own. Other plants make spores that are carried away by wind or rain. When the spores land in a suitable place, they grow into new plants.

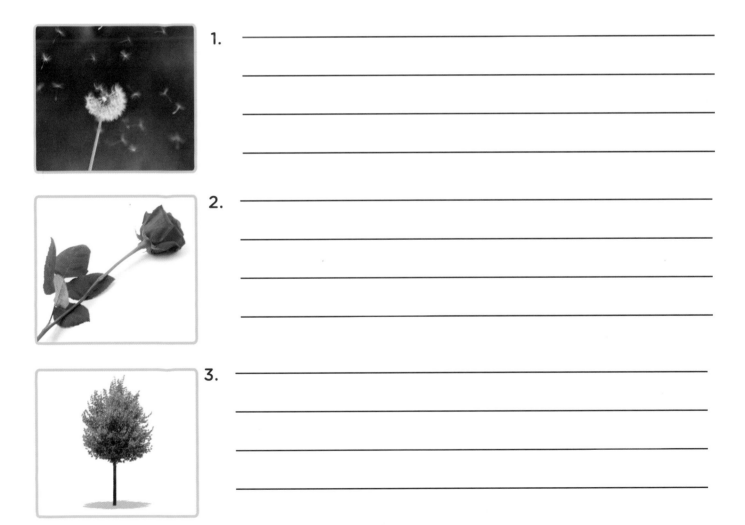

1. _____
_____
_____
_____

2. _____
_____
_____
_____

3. _____
_____
_____
_____

Showing Fractions

Divide each shape into the number of parts shown in the fraction.
Then shade the parts to show the fraction.

1.

$$\frac{5}{8}$$

2.

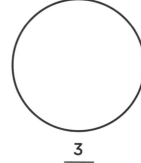

$$\frac{3}{6}$$

3.

$$\frac{4}{4}$$

4.

$$\frac{1}{4}$$

5.

$$\frac{1}{2}$$

6.

$$\frac{8}{12}$$

7.

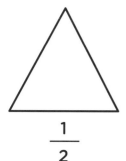

$$\frac{4}{10}$$

8.

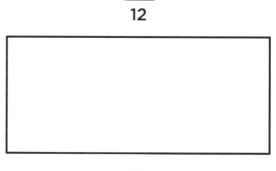

$$\frac{2}{8}$$

Where Are You?

Use the clues to find the answers. Write your answers in the puzzle.

starfish   beach   shells   ocean   sand   sunscreen

fire   touch   salty   stories   roast

Do you want to take a trip? We can go to the tide pools to hunt for yellow **[1 across]** and pink **[9 across]**. It's okay to look, but we must not **[6 down]**! My favorite thing to do is swim in the **[5 across]**. It feels cool and tastes **[8 down]**. Before you go in, make sure to put on some **[8 across]**. I love to feel the warm, wet **[3 down]** between my toes. We can use it to build a sandcastle. Later on, we can make a big **[7 across]**. We can **[2 down]** hot dogs and marshmallows. Then we can sit around it and tell **[1 down]**. Sounds like a great day at the **[4 down]**!

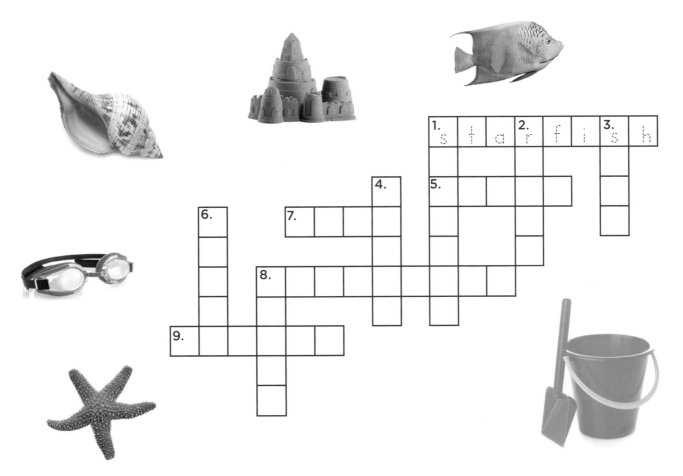

1. s t a r f i s h

Make a Difference

Good citizens follow rules and obey laws. They work to help make their communities better. They take good care of our planet Earth.
List some of the things that good citizens in your community do.

Follow rules and obey laws

_____

_____

_____

_____

_____

_____

_____

_____

_____

Take care of our planet Earth

_____

_____

_____

_____

_____

_____

_____

_____

Make communities better

_____

_____

_____

_____

_____

_____

_____

Fun at the Fair

Perimeter is the distance around a shape. Find the perimeter of each animal pen at the county fair.

1. _____

8 ft.
5 ft.
5 ft.
5 ft.
8 ft.

2. _____

3 ft.
3 ft.
3 ft.
3 ft.
3 ft.
3 ft.

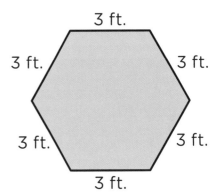

3. _____

3 m
2 m
1 m
2 m
3 m
4 m
5 m
4 m

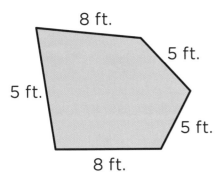

4. _____

5 ft.
5 ft.
5 ft.
5 ft.
5 ft.
5 ft.
5 ft.
5 ft.
5 ft.
5 ft.
5 ft.
5 ft.

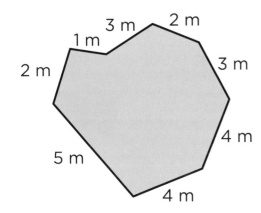
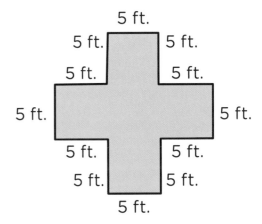

5. _____

6 m
6 m
10 m

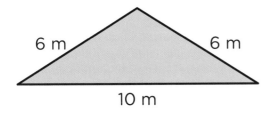
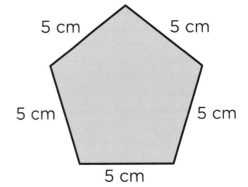

6. _____

5 cm
5 cm
5 cm
5 cm
5 cm

Strange Pets

Read the passages. Then answer the questions.

Pot-Bellied Pigs

Some people say that pot-bellied pigs make great pets. They can live right in your home, just like a dog or a cat. But they can also grow to weigh about 125 pounds! Pigs are very clean. They can even be trained to use a litter box. Owners claim their pigs are loving, smart, and playful. They also seem to share human feelings. Some owners say their pigs cry! Pot-bellied pigs are very smart. They are easy to train, much like the family dog. Pigs have been trained to play the piano, dance, and even ride a skateboard!

Skunks

Most people stay away from skunks because of their stinky spray. This spray comes from scent glands. To keep a skunk, you must have the scent glands removed. Skunk owners claim these animals are great pets. They say skunks are curious and playful. And they only grow to weigh between four and ten pounds. But skunks are hard to train. They're very smart but need a lot of attention. Most of all, keep a close eye on this pet. Skunks will steal anything they can get their paws on!

Name four ways these pets are different:

_____

_____

_____

_____

Name four ways these pets are alike:

_____

_____

_____

_____

Which pet would you like to have? Why? Write about it on another piece of paper.

Tell Me About It

Authors try to make their writing as interesting as possible. One way to do this is to describe sights, sounds, tastes, smells, and textures in detail. Write your own descriptions of the following experiences. Use as much detail as possible.

Eating cotton candy

_____

_____

_____

_____

Riding a Ferris wheel

_____

_____

_____

_____

Visiting a petting zoo

_____

_____

_____

_____

Watching a fireworks show

_____

_____

_____

_____

Patty's Pizza Palace

Read the menu below. Use the menu to solve each problem.

1. Jamie got 2 slices of pizza. The first slice had peppers and tomatoes. The other slice had ham. How much did he spend?

   $3.25 _____

MENU

Pizza, per slice (with cheese)
$1.00
Whole pizza (with cheese)
$6.00

TOPPINGS

Pepperoni	50¢	Peppers	45¢
Tomatoes	30¢	Onions	40¢
Mushrooms	35¢	Olives	25¢
		Ham	50¢

2. Maria got one slice of pizza with olives, ham, pepperoni, and tomatoes. She paid with three $1 bills. How much change did she get back?

   _____

3. Truc got a whole pizza for her family. It had pepperoni, olives, and mushrooms. How much did she spend?

   _____

4. Mali and Cris got a whole pizza to share. Mali chose onions and mushrooms. Cris added pepperoni and peppers. How much did they spend?

   _____

5. Amir got 3 slices of pizza. One slice had ham, one had tomatoes, and one had olives. He paid with a $5 bill. How much change did he get back?

   _____

6. Coach Dean got 2 whole pizzas for his baseball team. One had pepperoni and ham. The other pizza had onions and peppers. How much did he spend?

   _____

Write It Right

Rewrite each sentence correctly. Add correct punctuation and capital letters where needed.

1. fourth of july is my favorite holiday

_____

2. my brother jorge was born on april 16 2000

_____

3. have you read the book ramona the pest by beverly cleary

_____

4. aunt kathy moved to austin texas

_____

5. teds party was at noon last saturday september 10

_____

6. may i take reggie to play ball at hillside park

_____

7. did mr chase get a bus for our trip to the natural history museum

_____

8. david and his family went to camp black bear over labor day

_____

9. last summer my family visited the grand canyon in arizona

_____

10. mrs chin showed us pictures of blue whales jellyfish and eels

_____

Stick to the Topic

A **paragraph** is a group of sentences that all tell about one thing.
The **topic sentence** tells what the paragraph is about. The other
sentences give details about the main topic.

Read the topic sentence in the middle of the web. Complete the web
by writing sentences that support the topic sentence.

Going to the
county fair is fun.

Now use the sentences in the web to write a paragraph about going to the county
fair. Use as many details as you can to make your writing interesting.

_____

_____

_____

_____

_____

Look It Up

Which type of reference material would you use for the following information? Choose from the materials listed in the word box.

| dictionary | thesaurus | atlas | encyclopedia | almanac |

1. the meaning of the word **heifer** _dictionary_

2. the number of people who work on farms in your state _____

3. the history of the Ferris wheel _____

4. another word for **fair** _____

5. a map of your state _____

Answer the questions below by using the references at the top of the page.

6. What does **heifer** mean? _____

7. How many people in your state work on farms? _____

8. What is one interesting fact about the history of the Ferris wheel? _____
_____

9. What is another word for **fair** that has a similar meaning to "a gathering for people"? _____

10. What are the names of the some of the towns and cities around your community?
_____

Pick a Combo

Follow the directions below.

1. You can pick any two toppings you want at Iggy's Ice Cream Shop. The topping choices are: fudge, nuts, caramel, and chocolate chips.

List all of the possible topping combinations.

fudge and

_____

_____

_____

nuts and

_____

_____

caramel and

_____

2. At Candy Castle, you can pick any two candy combos for 50¢. The candy choices are: gummy worms, lemon drops, jelly beans, and mint swirls.

List the candy combinations.

gummy worms and

_____

_____

_____

lemon drops and

_____

_____

jelly beans and

_____

Same, but Different

Homophones are words that sound the same but are not spelled the same and mean something different.

Read each word below. Then write the word that names the picture. You can see that the words sound the same but are not spelled the same. They are homophones!

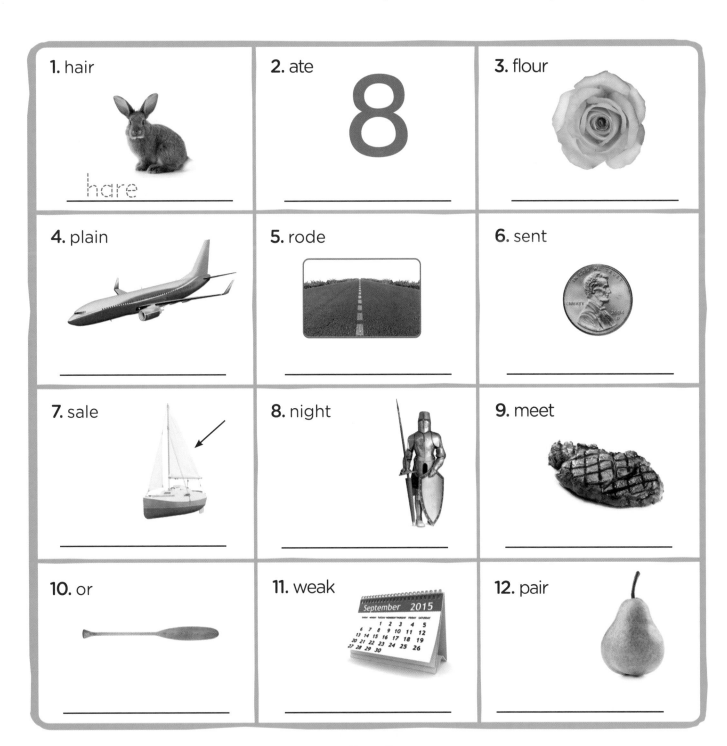

1. hair

hare

2. ate

8

_____

3. flour

_____

4. plain

_____

5. rode

_____

6. sent

_____

7. sale

_____

8. night

_____

9. meet

_____

10. or

_____

11. weak

September 2015

_____

12. pair

_____

Your Family

Your **ancestors** are members of your family who lived a long time ago.

Find out more about your ancestors by interviewing an adult. Ask where your ancestors came from. Ask to hear a story about and see a picture of your ancestors.

Write a paragraph about your ancestors. Then draw a picture below.

_____

_____

_____

_____

_____

_____

_____

_____

Perfect Paragraph

A **paragraph** begins with a **topic sentence**. This sentence tells what the paragraph is about. A **paragraph** also has a **main idea** and **supporting details**.

Read the following paragraph. Then go back and underline the topic sentence. Write the main idea and two supporting details below.

The water cycle is the way Earth recycles water. First, the sun warms water. Then the water dries up into the air. Cool air changes the water into vapor as it rises. Then the water vapor changes into water drops. These drops form clouds. The drops get colder. They get heavier and bigger. Finally, the drops are too heavy to stay in the clouds. They fall back to the earth as rain, snow, or hail.

The main idea is: _____

Two supporting details are:

_____

_____

Now, write your own paragraph. You can write about school, a pet, or anything else that interests you. Make sure to include:

• a topic sentence
• a main idea
• supporting details

_____

_____

_____

_____

_____

_____

_____

_____

Trivia Time

Match the names of heroes with their accomplishments.
Use reference material if you need help.

Thomas Jefferson

Harriet Tubman

Laura Ingalls Wilder

Abraham Lincoln

Frederick Douglass

Benjamin Franklin

Susan B. Anthony

Martin Luther King Jr.

Leader of the women's rights movement

Used the Underground Railroad to help slaves escape

16th president; wrote the Emancipation Proclamation to end slavery

Leader of the civil rights movement

3rd president; wrote the Declaration of Independence

Author and editor who spoke out against slavery

Inventor and patriot who helped with the American Revolution

Author of children's books about pioneer life

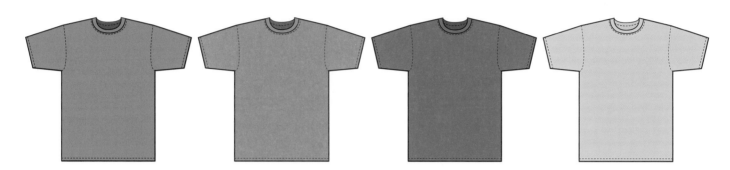

Choose a Color

Dana has 3 red shirts, 3 blue shirts, 2 green shirts, and 1 yellow shirt.
Dana has decided to play a game to decide which color to wear.
Follow the instructions to play Dana's game.

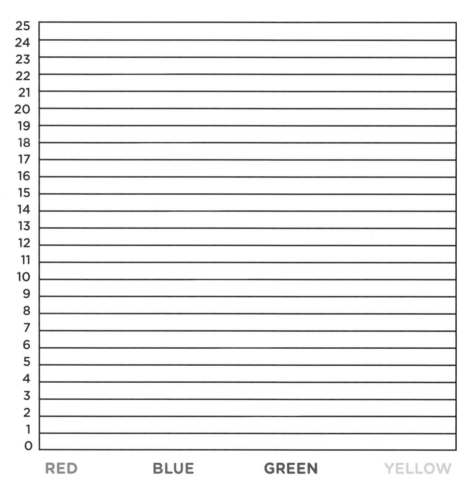

- Cut 3 red squares, 3 blue squares, 2 green squares, and 1 yellow square from colored paper.

- Place the squares in a paper bag.

- Draw one square at a time. Record the color on the graph and then put the square back into the bag.

- Repeat until you have drawn 50 squares.

- The color that is drawn the most is the color that Dana will wear to school.

1. Which color was chosen the most? _____

2. Which color was chosen the least? _____

3. Which two colors had an equal chance of being chosen? _____

Plot the Answer

Use the graph to find the answer to the riddle.
Write the letter that goes with each coordinate on the lines.

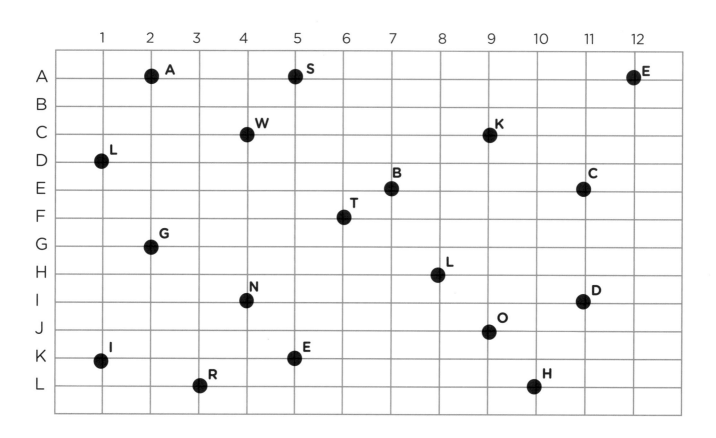

Riddle: Why do cows wear bells?

___ ___ ___ ___ ___   ___ ___ ___ ___ ___
(F,6) (L,10) (A,12) (K,1) (L,3)   (L,10) (J,9) (L,3) (I,4) (A,5)
                          ,

___ ___ ___   ___   ___ ___ ___ ___
(I,11) (J,9) (I,4)   (F,6)   (C,4) (J,9) (L,3) (C,9)

Mimi's Marvelous Muffins

Read the recipe. Then answer the questions below.

Muffins

Ingredients

2 cups flour
$\frac{1}{2}$ tsp salt
1 tsp baking powder
1 egg
1 stick butter
$\frac{2}{3}$ cup sugar
$\frac{3}{4}$ cup milk
2 cups blueberries

Preheat oven to 350°F. Mix all dry ingredients, except sugar. Beat butter, egg, milk, and sugar. Add dry ingredients to wet ingredients. Add blueberries. Place batter in a muffin tin. Use $\frac{1}{3}$ cup of batter per muffin cup. Bake for 25 to 30 minutes. Test muffins to make sure they're done. Stick a toothpick in a muffin. If it comes out clean, muffins are all done.

1. This recipe gives directions for making:
   a) cake
   b) muffins
   c) cookies

2. Which of these items is not needed to make this recipe?
   a) spoon
   b) bowl
   c) baking sheet

3. Which ingredient is added last to this recipe?
   a) sugar
   b) blueberries
   c) egg

4. What is the first step in this recipe?
   a) Mix together all the dry ingredients.
   b) Preheat oven to 350°F.
   c) Test muffins to make sure they're done.

5. What might be the next step in this recipe?
   a) Let muffins cool.
   b) Eat muffins.
   c) Put away ingredients.

School Supplies

Marcus is going shopping for school supplies. He has $40.00 to spend. Look at the school supplies below. Then answer the questions.

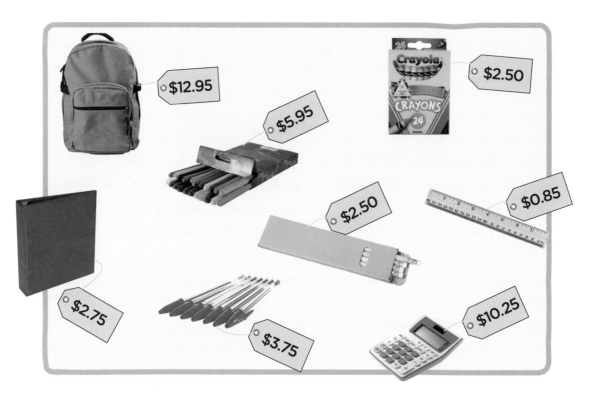

1. Marcus bought a backpack, a binder, and pens. How much did he spend?
   $12.95 + $ 2.75 + $ 3.75 = $19.45

   How much does he have left over? $40.00 - $19.45 = $20.55
2. Marcus bought crayons, a ruler, and a calculator. How much did he spend?

   _____

   How much does he have left over? _____
3. Marcus bought pencils, markers, and a binder. How much did he spend?

   _____

   How much does he have left over? _____
4. Marcus bought a binder, markers, and a ruler. How much did he spend?

   _____

   How much does he have left over? _____
5. Marcus bought a calculator, pens, and crayons. How much did he spend?

   _____

   How much does he have left over? _____

A New Beginning

Read the story. Then answer the questions.

The sun shines through Tina's window, and she wakes with a smile. Today is going to be a great day! Tina goes to her closet and picks out her very best school outfit. After she gets dressed, she puts her new notebooks and pencils into her backpack. Her dad serves pancakes and eggs for breakfast while her mom packs her lunch. Then her mom drives her to the first day of school. Tina sees her friend, Becca, in front of the school office. "Great news!" says Becca. "We're in the same class again!" The girls drop their backpacks near the classroom door and head out to the playground. Tina can't wait for the bell to ring. Third grade is going to be fantastic!

1. Why do you think Tina wakes up with a smile?

_____

_____

2. What does Tina do to get ready for school?

_____

_____

3. What is special about this day?

_____

_____

4. Who is Becca?

_____

_____

5. What is Becca's good news?

_____

_____

6. What grade is Tina in?

_____

_____

Number Lines

Look at each number line. It shows a pattern. Complete the pattern by writing the numbers above the dots on the number line.

1.
```
0    3    6    9    12   15   18
```

2.
```
4    6    8    10
```

3.
```
0    4    8    12
```
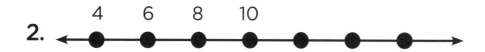

4.
```
20   18   16   14   12
```

5.
```
5    10   15   20
```

6.
```
30   26   22   18
```

7.
```
0    10   20   30
```

8.
```
1    2    4    8
```

Understanding Poetry

Read the passage. It is part of a poem called "The Walrus and the Carpenter" by Lewis Carroll. Then answer the questions.

The sun was shining on the sea,
Shining with all his might:
He did his very best to make
The billows smooth and bright—
And this was odd, because it was
The middle of the night.

The moon was shining sulkily,
Because she thought the sun
Had no business to be there
After the day was done—
"It's very rude of him," she said,
"To come and spoil the fun!"

The sea was wet as wet could be,
The sands were dry as dry.
You could not see a cloud, because
No cloud was in the sky:
No birds were flying overhead—
There were no birds to fly.

1. What two objects act like people?

_____

2. Why was it odd for the sun to be shining?

_____

_____

3. Why could you not see a cloud?

_____

_____

4. Write the three rhyming words from the first verse:

_____

5. Which two adjectives are repeated in the last verse?

_____

_____

_____

The Reason for the Seasons

Read the story. Then answer the questions.

In most parts of the world the weather changes based on the seasons. Summer temperatures are the hottest and winter temperatures are the coldest. Spring and autumn temperatures are somewhere in-between. These changes in temperature repeat themselves year after year. Some people mistakenly believe that these temperature changes have to do with how close Earth is to the sun during different times of the year. Actually, the seasons occur because  the angle at which the sun's rays hit Earth. During part of the year, the northern part of Earth leans more directly toward the sun than the southern part of Earth. This means that it is summer in the North and winter in the South. Later, the position of Earth reverses and the southern part has summer while the northern part has winter.

Read the statements. Write **true** or **false**.

1. When it is summer in the northern part of Earth, it is winter in the southern part.

_____

2. Winter is the warmest season.

_____

3. Changes in temperature are completely unpredictable.

_____

4. The seasons change because of the angles at which the sun's rays hit Earth.

_____

5. Summer is the warmest season.

_____

6. Temperatures change during the year based on how close Earth is to the sun.

_____

Mix of Measures

Read each problem. Then circle your answer.

1. Nina needed new carpet. She measured her bedroom using

a) yards
b) inches
c) miles

2. Juelia was very sick. The thermometer showed

a) 5°F
b) 33°F
c) 103°F

3. Tom weighed a bag of apples in the store. He put them on a

a) measuring cup
b) scale
c) ruler

4. The vet weighed Annie's hamster. He weighed the hamster using

a) pounds
b) feet
c) ounces

5. Dad took us for a ride in his new car. When we got home, he said we drove 35

a) yards
b) miles
c) inches

6. Tad put on his winter coat and gloves. The thermometer showed

a) 90°F
b) 75°F
c) 2°F

7. Katie drew a picture in her notebook. She measured it for a frame using

a) inches
b) feet
c) ounces

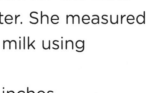

8. Mom needed $\frac{1}{2}$ cup of milk for the cake batter. She measured the milk using

a) inches
b) ounces
c) pounds

9. Gabe added a bit of salt to his soup. He used a

a) teaspoon
b) cup
c) ruler

Where Do I Find It?

Do you know how to find information? It can help you when you are reading or writing. Circle the correct reference for each question.

1. To find the week's sports scores, you should look in a
    a) dictionary
    b) encyclopedia
    c) newspaper

2. To find out where Japan is, you should look in an
    a) atlas
    b) thesaurus
    c) phone book

3. To find the page number for a chapter, you should look in the
    a) dictionary
    b) newspaper
    c) table of contents

4. To find the meaning of the word *timid*, you should look in a
    a) atlas
    b) dictionary
    c) encyclopedia

5. To find topics in a book, you should look in the
    a) index
    b) thesaurus
    c) title page

6. To find a synonym for the word *happy*, you should look in a
    a) thesaurus
    b) dictionary
    c) atlas

7. To find out about today's weather, you should look in a
    a) table of contents
    b) phone book
    c) newspaper

8. To research the history of ballet, you should look in an
    a) encyclopedia
    b) dictionary
    c) index

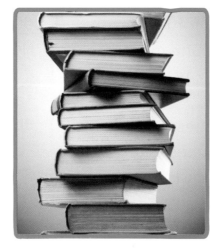

Where in the World?

Follow the directions below.

Have you ever wondered where the things that you buy come from? Some things may come from your local area. Others may come from other areas around the United States or from other countries. Most items have a label that tells where the item came from.

Collect the items below. Look at the packaging and the labels on the items to see if you can find out where they came from.

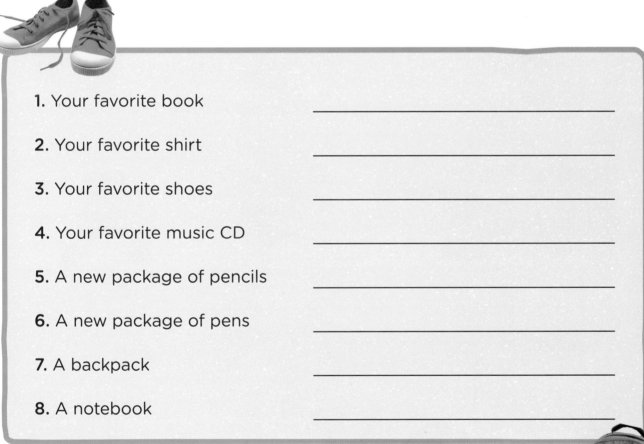

1. Your favorite book _____

2. Your favorite shirt _____

3. Your favorite shoes _____

4. Your favorite music CD _____

5. A new package of pencils _____

6. A new package of pens _____

7. A backpack _____

8. A notebook _____

What Are the Odds?

Predicting is an important math skill. It can help you come close to an answer without actually solving a problem. Read each problem carefully. Then circle the best answer.

1. You flip a quarter 10 times. About how many times will it be tails?

   a) 2 in 10
   b) 5 in 10
   c) 10 in 10

2. A jar contains 100 jelly beans. 60 are red, 20 are green, and 20 are purple. You take one jelly bean. What is the chance you will pick a green jelly bean?

   a) 6 in 10
   b) 2 in 10
   c) all the same

3. A bag contains 40 marbles. 16 are blue. You take one marble. What is the chance you will get a blue marble?

   a) 8 in 20
   b) 10 in 20
   c) 2 in 10

4. You have 16 pairs of socks. 3 pairs are black, 8 pairs are white, 5 pairs are brown. What is the chance you will grab a pair of white socks?

   a) 1 in 4
   b) 1 in 3
   c) 1 in 2

5. There are 12 ladybugs in the jar. 4 are red, 6 are orange, 2 are white. If you open the lid, what is the chance that a white bug will fly out?

   a) 6 in 12
   b) 1 in 6
   c) 1 in 4

6. You throw a 5 for your first roll of the die. What is the chance you will throw a 5 on your next roll?

   a) 1 in 5
   b) 2 in 5
   c) 1 in 6

Matching Meanings

Some words have several meanings.

Example

Tanya wants to <u>play</u> on the tennis team.
I saw a funny <u>play</u> last weekend.

Choose the sentence that has the same meaning as the underlined word in the first sentence. Circle the letter.

1. Mom held Brie's <u>hand</u> when they crossed the street.
   a) I cut my hand on the fence.
   b) Please hand me the apple.
   c) The crowd gave her a hand for her speech.

2. Did you go to the county <u>fair</u>?
   a) My teacher is fair when it comes to grades.
   b) The princess was known as fair and sweet.
   c) Mom won first prize for her pie at the fair.

3. Make sure to <u>check</u> your answers.
   a) Did you check whether the baby is asleep?
   b) Place a check next to each item you want.
   c) Dad wrote a check for my new bike.

4. Enzo's last name is hard to <u>spell</u>.
   a) Grandma laid down for a spell.
   b) How do you spell the word *tomorrow*?
   c) The fairy cast a magic spell over the prince.

5. My <u>back</u> is sore from carrying those boxes.
   a) Manny will back the car out of the garage.
   b) Jenny just got back from her trip.
   c) Bill felt the ball hit him in the back.

6. Kara got a new <u>lock</u> for her bike.
   a) Did you lock the back door?
   b) The lock on the gate was easy to open.
   c) Mom cut a lock of the baby's hair.

7. I added two eggs to the cake <u>batter</u>.
   a) Brownie batter is thick and sweet.
   b) Branches will batter the window in a storm.
   c) Steph is the best batter on our softball team.

8. A big <u>wave</u> crashed on the beach.
   a) I will wave to Joey on stage.
   b) Lin has a curly wave in her long hair.
   c) Can you surf on that big wave?

Secret Numbers

Read the clues to find the secret number.

1. It is an odd number.
It is in the triangle and in the square.
It is more than 6.
It is divisible by 3.
The secret number is: _____

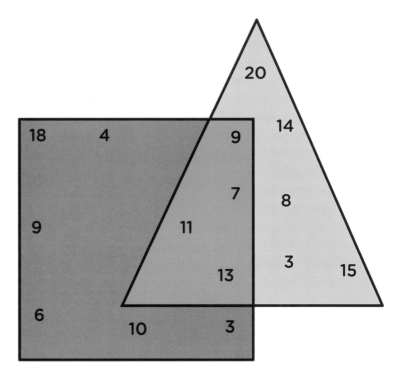

2. It is not an odd number.
It is in the circle.
It is less than 16.
It is divisible by 5.
The secret number is: _____

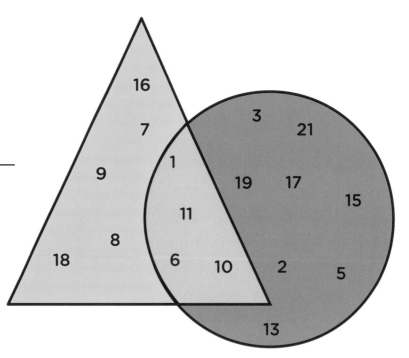

Howl in the Wind

Read the passage below. Then answer the questions.

Have you ever heard a wolf howl? It is a spooky sound. It is a lonely sound. Wolves make many kinds of sounds. They bark, woof, whine, and yelp. They also moan and growl. But when we think of wolves, we think of howling. Why do wolves howl?

The center of a wolf's life is its pack. Howling is the glue that keeps the pack together. You could say that the pack that howls together, stays together! Wolves wander over large areas to find food. They are often separated from one another. Of all their calls, howling is the only one that works over great distances. If you separate a wolf from its pack, it will soon begin howling over and over again.

There are two main reasons that wolves howl. They howl to keep the pack together. They also howl to keep enemies away. The enemies are usually other wolf packs. Wolves don't really howl at the moon. They howl to talk to each other.

1. Name three sounds wolves make, besides howls.

_____

2. What does a wolf howl sound like?

_____

3. What is the center of a wolf's life?

_____

4. Why might a wolf be away from its pack?

_____

5. What are the two main reasons wolves howl?

_____

_____

Baseball Season

Read about the baseball stadium. Then solve the problems.

The baseball stadium has 4,500 seats. There are:
- 700 seats in Section A
- 1,800 seats in Section B
- 1,200 seats in Section C
- 800 seats in Section D

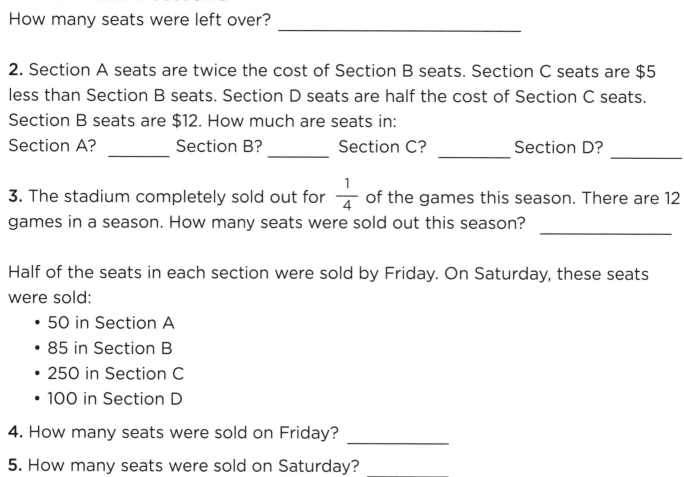

1. These seats were sold for the first game:
- 550 seats in Section A
- 1,200 seats in Section B
- 800 seats in Section C
- 730 seats in Section D

How many seats were left over? _____

2. Section A seats are twice the cost of Section B seats. Section C seats are $5 less than Section B seats. Section D seats are half the cost of Section C seats. Section B seats are $12. How much are seats in:

Section A? _____ Section B? _____ Section C? _____ Section D? _____

3. The stadium completely sold out for $\frac{1}{4}$ of the games this season. There are 12 games in a season. How many seats were sold out this season? _____

Half of the seats in each section were sold by Friday. On Saturday, these seats were sold:
- 50 in Section A
- 85 in Section B
- 250 in Section C
- 100 in Section D

4. How many seats were sold on Friday? _____

5. How many seats were sold on Saturday? _____

6. How many seats were sold all together? _____

How Do You Know?

When you read, knowing **who**, **what**, **when**, and **where** helps you understand what is happening in a story. Write *who*, *what*, *when*, or *where* for each phrase below.

1. in the forest _where_

2. my brother and I _____

3. a hungry bear _____

4. after sunset _____

5. ten colorful butterflies _____

6. a helpful forest ranger _____

7. over the mountain _____

8. early in the morning _____

9. at the same time _____

10. friendly campers _____

11. in the cool lake _____

12. on the steep trail _____

13. inside the tent _____

14. at the crackling campfire _____

15. after the thunderstorm _____

16. up the pine tree _____

17. his best friend _____

18. a newborn fawn _____

19. around the meadow _____

20. over the cliff _____

Switch It

Finish each multiplication sentence.

1. If 7 × 5 = 35 . . .   then 5 × 7 = 35.

2. If 3 × 12 = 36 . . .   then ☐ × 3 = 36.

3. If 5 × 4 = 20 . . .   then ☐ × 5 = 20.

4. If 11 × 6 = 66 . . .   then 6 × ☐ = 66.

5. If 8 × 3 = 24 . . .   then 3 × 8 = ☐.

6. If 6 × 7 = 42 . . .   then 7 × 6 = ☐.

7. If 9 × 5 = 45 . . .   then ☐ × 9 = 45.

8. If 8 × 10 = 80 . . .   then 10 × ☐ = 80.

9. If 12 × 11 = 132 . . .   then 11 × ☐ = 132.

10. If 9 × 6 = 54 . . .   then ☐ × 9 = 54.

11. If 2 × 5 = 10 . . .   then 5 × 2 = ☐.

12. If 4 × 12 = 48 . . .   then 12 × ☐ = 48.

Answer Key

Page 4
2. 54
3. 143
4. 100
5. 117
6. 165
7. 353
8. 804
9. 781
10. 905
11. 978
12. 600

Page 5
Nouns are placed in the story in this order: ant, stream, leaf, tree, bird, stick, hunter, foot, woods, heart.

Page 6
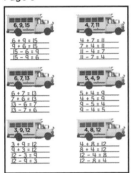

Page 7
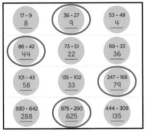

Page 8
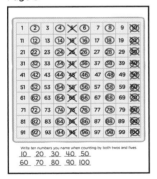

Page 9
These are the circled sentences:
4. Everyone will dance.
6. We will serve burgers and chips.
7. We hope you can come.
Answers to questions 9 and 10 will vary.

Page 10
2. ten, huge, colorful; 3
3. one, striped; 2
4. tall, brown, green; 3
5. yellow; 1
6. small, furry; 2
7. sour, bad; 2
8. sweet, little, funny; 3
9. best; 1
10. red, yellow; 2

Page 11
scissors
metal measuring spoon
metal paper clip
belt buckle

Page 12
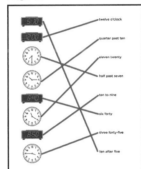

Page 13
1. 5, 4, 2, 1, 3
2. 1, 3, 5, 4, 2
3. 5, 1, 3, 4, 2

Page 14
2, 6, 4, 3, 1, 5
Designs will vary.

Page 15
2.
3.
4.
5.
6.

Page 16
2. 25¢, 25¢, 25¢, 10¢, 10¢
3. 10¢, 5¢, 5¢, 5¢, 1¢
4. 25¢, 25¢, 25¢, 5¢

Page 17
2. bite
3. track
4. rust
5. thing
6. street
7. drop
8. brake
Page is complete when lines are drawn between circled words to show a path between the cat and the mouse.

Page 18
These bills and coins should be circled:
2. one five-dollar bill, one dollar bill, one quarter, two dimes, five pennies
3. six quarters, two dimes, one nickel
4. three dollar bills, two nickels, five pennies

Page 19
Answers will vary.

Page 20
1. Two bugs are circled.
2. Five bugs are circled.
3. Six bugs are circled.
4. Six bugs are circled.
5. One bug is circled.
6. Six bugs are circled.

Page 21
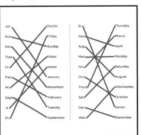

Page 22
2. The directions to the lake were unclear.
3. Then Dad replaced the map in his backpack.
4. Mom and Dad were unhappy about being lost on the trail.
5. "We should have previewed our route," said Mom.
6. "You're right," said Dad. "We are unprepared for this."

Page 23
2. Chapter 1
3. page 60
4. places to eat
5. the chapter about beaches
6. Sports
7. page 80
8. Chapter 5

Page 24
2. 15 − 7 = 8
3. 15 − 10 = 5
4. 15 − 3 = 12
5. 15 − 6 = 9
6. 15 − 8 = 7
7. 15 − 5 = 10
8. 15 − 9 = 6

Page 25
2. The caves began forming millions of years ago.
3. The caves are made from limestone.
4. These are called stalactites.
5. Answers will vary.

Page 26
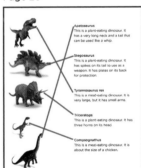

Page 27
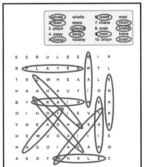

Page 28
Sentences that should be circled:
3, 5, and 6.
Sentences that should be crossed
out: 2 and 4.

Page 29
2. <
3. <
4. <
5. >
6. >
7. <
8. >
9. =
10. <
11. >
12. >

Page 30
2. more
3. less
4. less
5. more
6. more
7. less
8. less
9. more
10. less
11. less
12. less
13. more
14. less
15. less
16. more

Page 31
2. 3
3. 1
4. 3
5. Cheetah Cabin
6. Bobcat Cabin, Donkey Cabin

Page 32
2. 16, 32, 128, 256
3. 12, 16, 28, 32
4. 40, 55
5. 250, 400, 450
6. 80, 60, 40
7. 24, 15, 6
8. 390, 370, 350

Page 33
2. ounces
3. ounces
4. pounds
5. ounces
6. pounds
7. ounces
8. pounds
9. ounces

Page 34
1. Spiders are arachnids.
2. Spiders eat insects.
3. Baby spiders are called
spiderlings.
4. They help people by eating
harmful insects.

Page 35
2. walked
3. low
4. quiet
5. few
Answers to questions 6–11 will
vary.

Page 36
Letter will vary.

Page 37
2. 22, 23
3. 65, 19
4. 17, 51
5. 13, 14
6. 46, 50
7. 16, 28
8. 62, 13
9. 33, 19

Page 38

Page 39
4, 5, 3, 1, 2
1, 5, 2, 4, 3

Page 40
1. 9
2. 24
3. 12
4. 8
5. 20
6. 5

Page 41
2. doorknob
3. seashell
4. keyboard
5. barefoot
6. postcard
7. shoelace
8. peanut
9. pancake
10. sunshine
snake shake

Page 42
2. Cowboy shirts, ties
3. hula hoop
4. sock hop
5. Dance cards

Page 43
2. 16 + 22 + 15 = 53
3. 30 × 3 = Jenna practices for 90
minutes per week.
60 hours = 360 minutes
360 ÷ 90 = 4
Jenna needs to practice for 4
weeks.
4. 12, 14, 16, 18, 20, 22, 24, 26, 28,
30
The tenth ball will go 30 feet.

Page 44
Across:
1. 14
4. 6
6. 3
7. 9
8. 20
Down:
2. 12
3. 18
4. 16
5. 4
8. 10

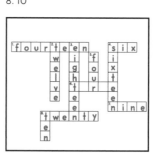

Page 45
2. bakes, baked
3. bark, barked
4. gallop, galloped
5. move, moved
6. want, wanted
7. talk, talked
8. visit, visited
9. play, played
10. crawl, crawled

Page 46
2. Game 3 and Game 6
3. 11 runs
4. 17 runs

Page 47
2. Mrs.
3. Ave.
4. Sat.
5. Wed.
6. Dr.
7. Dr.
8. Aug.

Page 48
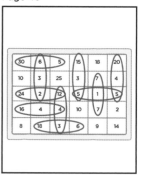

Page 49
Circle:
home
clock
snow
smoke
soap
throw
rock
drove
roast
2. roast
3. throw
4. snow
5. clock
6. drove
7. soap
8. home
9. smoke
10. rock

Page 50
2. Casey was excited.
3. She was nervous that she would
land on her belly or crash her head
on the bottom of the pool.
4. Casey was happy.
5. chuckled

Page 51
Sentences that should be circled:
3 and 6.
Sentences that should be crossed
out: 2, 4, and 5.

Page 52

Page 53
2. We'll
3. didn't
4. I'm
5. aren't
6. don't
7. haven't
8. isn't
9. Here's
10. I'll

Page 54
2. 26 + 34 = 60; 60 − 26 = 34
3. 75 + 12 = 87; 87 − 75 = 12
4. 18 + 39 = 57; 57 − 18 = 39
5. 69 + 24 = 93; 93 − 69 = 24
6. 35 + 15 = 50; 50 − 35 = 15
7. 47 + 28 = 75; 75 − 47 = 28
8. 29 + 29 = 58; 58 − 29 = 29
9. 61 + 24 = 85; 85 − 61 = 24
10. 17 + 39 = 56; 56 − 17 = 39
11. 63 + 32 = 95; 95 − 63 = 32
12. 55 + 17 = 72; 72 − 55 = 17
BECAUSE THEY CAN'T CARRY A SUITCASE

Page 55
2. 4
3. 120
4. 1
5. 14
6. 56
7. 6
8. 2

Page 56
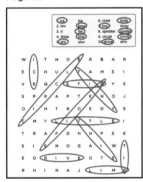

Page 57
1. 518
2. 110
3. 280
4. 159
5. 91
6. 141
7. 332
8. 390
9. 187
10. 409
11. 288
12. 387

Page 58
2. 103
3. 8
4. 14
5. flamingos and ostriches
6. b

Page 59
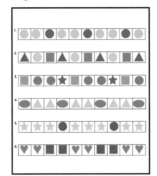

Page 60
1. Meg's new shoes are red.
2. Meg plays softball.
3. She knew her shoes were special right away.
4. On Meg's way home, she flew.
5. Answers will vary.

Page 61
Sentences will be similar to these:
2. We saw lions, tigers, and bears.
3. I liked the tigers the best, but my brother liked the bears better.
4. After lunch we went to see the monkeys and the polar bears.
5. We shopped at the gift shop before we left and my brother and I bought T-shirts.
6. I was sad to leave the zoo because I wanted to stay longer.

Page 62
2. .
3. ?
4. ?
5. .
6. !
Sentences will vary.

Page 63
Poems will vary.

Page 64
The white-winged duck is a bird.
The whooping crane is a bird.
The silver shark is a fish.
The African elephant is a mammal.
The blue whale is a mammal.

Page 65
2. lions
3. gorillas
4. You head southeast to get from the gorillas to the giraffes. Then continue southeast to get to the elephants.

Page 66
2. no
3. yes
4. no
5. yes

Page 67
2. zebras
3. foxes
4. friends
5. snakes
6. bunches
7. rocks
8. bunnies
9. bushes
10. babies

Page 68
2. White House
3. Liberty Bell
4. "The Star-Spangled Banner"
5. flag
6. Statue of Liberty

Page 69
2. 35
3. 48
4. 27
5. 30

Page 70
2. chocolate
3. 5
4. 4
5. 32 people
6. Answers will vary.

Page 71
2. knows; knew
3. breaks; broke
4. feels; felt
5. swings; swung
6. travel; traveled
7. makes; made
8. throws; threw
9. feeds; fed
10. draws; drew

Page 72
2. 3
3. 9
4. 8
5. 3
6. 11

Page 73
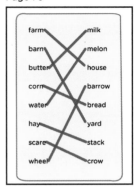

2. barnyard
3. buttermilk
4. cornbread
5. watermelon
6. haystack
7. scarecrow
8. wheelbarrow

Page 74
1. or
2. $\frac{3}{6}$ $\frac{1}{2}$
3. $\frac{1}{3}$ or
4. $\frac{2}{8}$ $\frac{1}{4}$
5. $\frac{1}{4}$ or
6. $\frac{5}{10}$ or $\frac{1}{2}$
7. $\frac{3}{3}$
8. $\frac{5}{6}$ or 1
9. $\frac{4}{4}$
$\frac{8}{9}$

Page 75
Circle:
spell
wheel
peach
dear
three
street
clean
dead
eel
went
2. went
3. peach
4. dead
5. street
6. eel
7. three
8. dear
9. wheel
10. clean

Page 76
In July, Becky and Jim visited Aunt Tonya's farm. On their first day there, they swam in Sunstone Creek. Afterward, they hiked up Butler's Hill. The next day they collected eggs! Aunt Tonya said they could sell the eggs at the farmers' market on Main Street. On Saturday, they helped clean the horse stalls before their riding lessons. That evening, Aunt Tonya took everyone on a hayride. Becky and Jim had a great time on the farm.

Page 77
1. b
2. a
3. d
4. b
5. b

Page 78
2. 40¢; forty
3. 55¢; fifty-five
4. 31¢; thirty-one
5. 64¢; sixty-four
6. 86¢; eighty-six
7. 42¢; fourty-two
8. 90¢; ninety
Jefferson

Page 79
1. Circle: First, tiny seedlings. Azra knew that soon pink and purple. Soon, big flowers!
2. Circle: Are Asian and African. Have five front toes. Like elephants?
3. Circle: Got a snowboard for his birthday. Over the snow really fast! Rides better and better.
4. Circle: All the planets. Trip to the moon. To my family.
5. Answers will vary, but all sentences should be complete.

Page 80
Answers will vary.

Page 81
2. hiking
3. baseball
4. boating
5. biking

Page 82
1. c
2. a
3. a
4. c
5. a

Page 83
2. 3,540; 3,640; 3,740; 3,840; 3,940; 4,040
3. 405; 435; 465; 495; 525; 555
4. 1,425; 1,675; 1,925; 2,175; 2,425; 2,675
5. 7,000; 7,500; 8,000; 8,500; 9,000; 9,500
6. 3,372; 4,372; 5,372; 6,372; 7,372; 8,372

Page 84
2. Train 10
3. 2 hours and 45 minutes
4. 30 minutes
5. 2 hours
6. 2:00 PM

Page 85
2. Wow, there are many, many stars in the sky! E
3. Nine planets are in our solar system. T
4. Would you like to go to the moon? A
5. Bring moon rocks back from your trip. C
6. Get ready to ride the fast rocket. C
7. Mars is called the red planet. T
8. Is the sun a planet or a star? A
9. Never look at the sun. C
10. How many rings are around Saturn? A

Page 86
2. 6,000 + 700 + 30 + 2
3. 8,000 + 300 + 80 + 8
4. 3,000 + 900 + 50 + 4
5. 2,000 + 500 + 40 + 2
6. 4,000 + 300 + 20 + 0
7. 5,000 + 500 + 50 + 5
8. 7,000 + 0 + 20 + 1

Page 87
1. b
2. c
3. b
4. a

Page 88
Answers will vary.

Page 89
The page is complete when all the letters are traced.

Page 90
HE QUACKS UP

Page 91

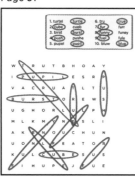

Page 92
The constellations got their names based on how they look in the sky.

Page 93
1. Each had different natural resources with which to build their homes.
2. The Northwest Indians and Eastern Woodland Indians lived in similar homes. This is probably because they had wood to use to build their homes.
3. The Plains Indians moved around the most. They could easily take their tepees with them when they moved.

Page 94
2. 4, 12, 24, 32
3. 16, 40, 80, 96
4. 20, 40, 90, 120

Page 95
Answers will vary.

Page 96
Answers will vary.

Page 97
1. 12
2. 24
3. 25
4. 18
5. 4
6. 40
7. 42
8. 10
9. 21
10. 16
11. 8
12. 45

Page 98
1. 8,000 + 200 + 90 + 5
2. 1,000 + 0 + 40 + 7
3. 9,000 + 900 + 60 + 2
4. 6,000 + 800 + 10 + 3
5. 359, 395, 539, 593, 935, 953
Circle: 359
Cross out: 953
6. 268, 286, 628, 682, 826, 862
Circle: 268
Cross out: 862

Page 99

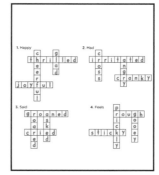

Page 100
2. 4
3. 3
4. 4
5. 5
6. 5
7. 10
8. 3
9. 3
10. 4
11. 5
12. 3

Page 101
2. Underline: fiery, flaming, scorching, sweaty
Circle: chilly, cold, frosty, frozen
3. Underline: glistening, glittery, glimmering, shimmering
Circle: dark, dim, gloomy, murky
4. Answers will vary.
5. Answers will vary.
6. before
7. cold
8. odor

Page 102
1. 35
2. 25
3. 25
4. 10
5. 75
6. 100

Page 103
Answers will vary.

Page 104
2. He was thoughtless and had drifted out to deep water.
3. A sailor was careful when he tossed the life jacket.
4. "I am thankful that you rescued me," he said.
5. The lifeguard told him that he should hire a swimming teacher.
6. "You have been so helpful," said the swimmer.

Page 105
Answers will vary.

Page 106

Page 107
Letters will vary.

Page 108
2. The tides are created by the force of gravity between the moon, Earth, and the sun.
3. The tides are different because the force of gravity between Earth, the moon, and the sun are not always the same.
4. Spring tides are when the tides come in very high and then go back out to sea very far. They occur when the moon, Earth, and the sun are in line with each other.
5. Neap tides occur when the moon, Earth, and the sun are at right angles to each other.

Page 109

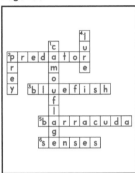

Page 110
1. 8 in.
2. 20 in.
3. 14 in.
4. 10 cm
5. 24 in.
6. 18 cm

Page 111
1. Underline: I sat by the window so I could watch the world go by. We crossed over a river. When we passed through the train stations, people waved at me! I waved back with a big smile on my face.
2. Underline: It can be rain. It can be spray from a garden hose. It can come from a water fountain.
3. Answers will vary.

Page 112
2. 36,573
3. 84,218
4. 94,203
5. 2,069
6. 7,531

Page 113
2. Keri 4, Ana 1, Ahmad 2, Juan 3
3. 48 coins

Page 114
Articles will vary.

Page 115
2. 10 cents
3. 60 cents
4. 40 cents
5. 32 cents
6. 30 cents
7. 45 cents
8. 40 cents

Page 116

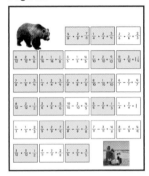

Page 117
2. bicycle
3. unhappy
4. underground
5. overpaid
6. unable
7. multicolored
8. miscount
9. nonstop
10. reheat
New words will vary.
Sentences will vary.

Page 118
2. clothes, choose
3. bear, fur
4. ate, fir
5. close, creak
6. chews, eight
Pictures will vary.

Page 119
Answers will vary.

Page 120
2. biggest
3. longer
4. tallest
5. stronger
6. faster
7. brighter
8. funniest
9. harder
10. shortest
11. and 12. Sentences will vary.

Page 121
Answers will vary.

Page 122

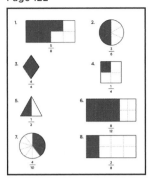

Page 123

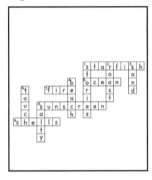

Page 124
Answers will vary.

Page 125
1. 31 ft.
2. 18 ft.
3. 24 m
4. 60 ft.
5. 22 m
6. 25 cm

Page 126
Four ways these pets are different:
Pigs weigh more than skunks.
Pigs are easier to train than skunks.
Pigs have human-like feelings.
Skunks steal.
Skunks have sweat glands.
Four ways these pets are alike:
Both have four legs.
Both make great pets
Both are smart.
Both are playful.

Page 127
Answers will vary.

Page 128
2. 45¢
3. $7.10
4. $7.70
5. 95¢
6. $13.85

Page 129
1. Fourth of July is my favorite holiday.
2. My brother Jorge was born on April 16, 2000.
3. Have you read the book Ramona the Pest, by Beverly Cleary?
4. Aunt Kathy moved to Austin, Texas.
5. Ted's party was at noon last Saturday, September 10.
6. May I take Reggie to play ball at Hillside Park?
7. Did Mr. Chase get a bus for our trip to the Natural History Museum?
8. David and his family went to Camp Black Bear over Labor Day.
9. Last summer my family visited the Grand Canyon in Arizona.
10. Mrs. Chin showed us pictures of blue whales, jellyfish, and eels.

Page 130
Answers will vary.

Page 131
2. almanac
3. encyclopedia
4. thesaurus
5. atlas
6. *Heifer* is another word for *cow*.
7.–10. Answers will vary.

Page 132
1. fudge and nuts, fudge and caramel, fudge and chocolate chips
nuts and caramel, nuts and chocolate chips
caramel and chocolate chips
2. gummy worms and lemon drops, gummy worms and jelly beans, gummy worms and mint swirls
lemon drops and jelly beans, lemon drops and mint swirls
jelly beans and mint swirls

Page 133
2. eight
3. flower
4. plane
5. road
6. cent
7. sail
8. knight
9. meat
10. oar
11. week
12. pear

Page 134
Paragraphs and pictures will vary.

Page 135

Topic sentence: The water cycle is the way Earth recycles water.
Main idea: The water cycle recycles water.
Two supporting details: Details will vary, but should include any two sentences after the topic sentence.
Paragraphs will vary.

Page 136

Thomas Jefferson	Leader of the Women's Rights Movement
Harriet Tubman	Used the Underground Railroad to help slaves escape
Laura Ingalls Wilder	16th president; wrote the Emancipation Proclamation to end slavery
Abraham Lincoln	Leader of the Civil Rights Movement
Frederick Douglass	3rd president; wrote the Declaration of Independence
Benjamin Franklin	Author and editor who spoke out against slavery
Susan B. Anthony	Inventor and patriot who helped with the American Revolution
Martin Luther King Jr.	Author of children's books about pioneer life

Page 137

Answers to 1 and 2 will vary.
3. red and blue

Page 138

THEIR HORNS DON'T WORK

Page 139

1. b
2. c
3. b
4. b
5. a

Page 140

2. $13.60, $26.40
3. $11.20, $28.80
4. $9.55, $30.45
5. $16.50, $23.50

Page 141

1. Tina is excited for the first day of school.
2. Tina picks an outfit, gets notebooks and pencils, and eats breakfast to get ready for school.
3. Today is special because it is the first day of third grade.
4. Becca is Tina's friend.
5. Becca's good news is that she and Tina are in the same class.
6. Tina is in third grade.

Page 142

2. 12, 14, 16
3. 16, 20, 24
4. 10, 8, 6, 4
5. 25, 30, 35, 40
6. 14, 10, 6, 2
7. 40, 50, 60, 70
8. 16, 32, 64

Page 143

1. the sun and the moon
2. It was the middle of the night.
3. No cloud was in the sky.
4. might, bright, night
5. wet, dry

Page 144

1. true
2. false
3. false
4. true
5. true
6. false

Page 145

1. a
2. c
3. b
4. c
5. b
6. c
7. a
8. b
9. a

Page 146

1. c
2. a
3. c
4. b
5. a
6. a
7. c
8. a

Page 147

Answers will vary.

Page 148

1. b
2. b
3. a
4. c
5. b
6. c

Page 149

1. a
2. c
3. a
4. b
5. c
6. b
7. a
8. c

Page 150

1. 9
2. 10

Page 151

1. Answers include: bark, woof, whine, yelp, moan, growl
2. A wolf's howl sounds spooky and lonely.
3. The center of a wolf's life is its pack.
4. A wolf might be away from its pack to find food.
5. Wolves howl to keep the pack together and to keep enemies away.

Page 152

1. 1,220 seats
2. Section A: $24, Section B: $12, Section C: $7, Section D: $3.50
3. 13,500 seats
4. 2,250 seats
5. 485 seats
6. 2,735 seats

Page 153

2. who
3. what
4. when
5. what
6. who
7. where
8. when
9. when
10. who
11. where
12. where
13. where
14. what
15. when
16. where
17. who
18. what
19. where
20. where

Page 154

2. 12
3. 4
4. 11
5. 24
6. 42
7. 5
8. 8
9. 12
10. 6
11. 10
12. 4

WEEK 1
COMPLETE!

★ PERFECT!   ★ PERFECT!   ★ PERFECT!   ★ PERFECT!

WEEK 2
COMPLETE!

WEEK 3
COMPLETE!

★ PERFECT!   ★ PERFECT!   ★ PERFECT!   ★ PERFECT!

WEEK 4
COMPLETE!

WOW!   WOW!   WOW!   WOW!

WEEK 5
COMPLETE!

WOW!   WOW!   WOW!   WOW!

WEEK 6
COMPLETE!

SUPER!   SUPER!   SUPER!   SUPER!

WEEK 7
COMPLETE!

SUPER!   SUPER!   SUPER!   SUPER!

WEEK 8
COMPLETE!

FANTASTIC!   FANTASTIC!   FANTASTIC!   FANTASTIC!

WEEK 9
COMPLETE!

WELL DONE!   WELL DONE!   WELL DONE!   WELL DONE!

WEEK 10
COMPLETE!

Excellent Work!   Excellent Work!   Excellent Work!   Excellent Work!

YOU'RE A STAR!   YOU'RE A STAR!   YOU'RE A STAR!   YOU'RE A STAR!   YOU'RE A STAR!

Excellent Work!	Excellent Work!	Excellent Work!	Excellent Work!	Excellent Work!
Excellent Work!	Excellent Work!	Excellent Work!	Excellent Work!	Excellent Work!
GREAT JOB!	GREAT JOB!	GREAT JOB!	GREAT JOB!	GREAT JOB!
GREAT JOB!	GREAT JOB!	GREAT JOB!	GREAT JOB!	GREAT JOB!
Hard Worker!	Hard Worker!	Hard Worker!	Hard Worker!	Hard Worker!
Hard Worker!	Hard Worker!	Hard Worker!	Hard Worker!	Hard Worker!
TERRIFIC WORK!	TERRIFIC WORK!	TERRIFIC WORK!	TERRIFIC WORK!	TERRIFIC WORK!
TERRIFIC WORK!	TERRIFIC WORK!	TERRIFIC WORK!	TERRIFIC WORK!	TERRIFIC WORK!
YOU'RE A STAR!	YOU'RE A STAR!	YOU'RE A STAR!	YOU'RE A STAR!	YOU'RE A STAR!